GW01006372

Water HOUSE

Water HOUSE

Edited by Felix Flesche

Texts by Christian Burchard and Felix Flesche

PRESTEL

MUNICH · BERLIN · LONDON · NEW YORK

Contents

Submerging Architecture

1234

Introduction

1234

Vision of Atlantis based on Plato's description

The Principality of Sealand, an independent state about ten kilometers off the eastern shores of Great Britain

In our time, water as life's origin symbolizes—despite ecological catastrophes—the dream of living in a symbiotic relationship with nature, much closer than would ever be possible on dry land. The oceans have an abundance of resources, unlimited energy reserves, and a seemingly endless supply of foodstuffs. Goods can be transported along a network of waterways that have to be neither constructed nor maintained. Town planners, architects, technicians, scientists, visionaries, inventors, and individualists have started to explore the utopian realms of water as a place to live. Dwellings, settlements, and cities for hundreds of thousands of inhabitants are already on the drawing board.

The futuristic designs of water cities with names like Aquapolis, Hydropolis, or Autopia (pages 92, 108, and 36) occupy the margins between dream and reality; between faith in the future progress of bionics, and memories of sunken cities and cultures that existed in harmony with the water. The epitome of fantastic island cultures is the myth of Atlantis, which stubbornly refuses to go away in spite of what scientists tell us, serving not only to inspire sci-fi authors but also many others with a pioneering spirit. Atlantis was the name given to the first United States vessel dedicated to oceanographic research; significantly, it was also given to an American space shuttle.

Our only historical source on Atlantis is Plato's *Timaeus* dialogue, a dispute between Greek scholars and Socrates, during which Plato's thoughts on an ideal state are discussed. We learn here that Athens was attacked more than 9,000 years ago by the inhabitants of Atlantis: "Now in this island of Atlantis there was a great and wonderful empire which had rule over the whole island and several others and over parts of the continent...This vast power, gathered into one, endeavored to subdue at a blow our country..." (*Selected Dialogues of Plato* [New York: Modern Library, 2001], 20d–27b). The people of Athens were protected by the sea god Poseidon, one of the mightiest gods of antiquity. The circular capital on the island was divided into districts by concentric rings of water. A canal connected these rings with the sea so that ships could pass from the open water directly to the glittering gold and silver royal fortress in the center. An echo of this ideal city lingers on in Meinhard von Gerkan's drawing board designs for the city of Luchao in China (page 34).

The myth of Atlantis has persisted as a symbol for the longing of life in accordance with nature and cosmic constellations. Subdued during the Industrialisation, it regained new strength in the anti-establishment and anti-technological protest movement of the 1960s. It is reflected in the musical *Hair* which celebrates a new age of peace ruled by Aquarius, and in the dreams of the Beatles of a life under the sea in their "Yellow Submarine". Donovan's nostalgic song "Atlantis" sums up this feeling for a whole generation:

The continent of Atlantis was an island
Which lay before the great flood
In the area we now call the Atlantic Ocean.
So great an area of land,
That from her western shores
Those beautiful sailors journeyed

Vito Acconci's Murinsel in Graz, Austria

Illustration from the children's book "Jäpkes Insel" (Jäpke's Island) by Lenore Gaul

To the South and the North Americas with ease,
In their ships with painted sails.
To them East Africa was a neighbor,
Across a short strait of sea miles.
. . . .
Way down below the ocean where I wanna be.

Islands

The idea of Atlantis is closely connected with the concept of Utopia, first described by Thomas More in his eponymous novel of 1516. Here, too, the place in question is an island, in fact an ideal island, which becomes the stage for an exemplary community life. More's literary concept was copied by numerous imitators. In the 17th century, the English philosopher Francis Bacon portrayed a social state on an island named New Atlantis situated nowhere in the known world, a utopia in the literal sense (the Greek *utopie* means "no place"). In the industrial age, the dream of artificial islands came together with a belief in the unlimited potential of technology. Jules Verne's *Propeller Island*, seven kilometers long and five kilometers wide, became the model for projects ranging from floating cities in the open seas to present-day projects such as AZ Island and Freedom Ship (pages 94–7). In view of the success of the man-made palm islands off Dubai (pages 40), it seems fair to say that the longing to live on islands has never gone away.

Whether these islands are for the super-rich or for all social groups, like the coral archipelago Arche Saya (page 36), in the background there is always the hope that life in an autarkic, miniature state will bring with it greater personal and political freedom. It seems that the inhabitants of the metropolises on terra firma project their longing for greater independence onto the wide-open spaces of the sea and its islands. "Water is freedom" could be the rallying cry of a future generation, leaving the confines of the big cities in order to reinvent civilization, starting from a historical zero. Outside territorial waters, the high seas have the considerable appeal of a no-man's land without any form of legal jurisdiction. In 1967, a strong-willed British subject took possession of a deserted island fortress off the coast of England, proclaimed it as the Principality of Sealand, and has since successfully defended his right to run the island as an independent state.

An unusual position is occupied by the building of the Murinsel in Graz, Austria, in accordance with plans made by Vito Acconci and Robert Punkenhofer in 2003. An artificial island is firmly anchored to the riverbed and connected to the two banks of the River Mur by bridges. The half-closed steel and glass construction looks like a whirlpool and combines a café, a theater, and a playground. The designers and engineers involved in this project have succeeded—very unusually—in combining a real-life social and cultural forum with the island dream.

Water

Water covers almost two-thirds of the Earth. What that means is demonstrated by photographs of the blue planet taken from outer space. From that distance the continents look like islands in a huge ocean that spans the entire globe. However, the proportions are

Noah's Ark in a woodcarving by Jost Ammann, 1567

Scenes from the film "Waterworld", 1995

deceptive because we are talking here only of the Earth's surface. If we imagine the planet Earth as a sphere with a diameter of seventy centimeters, the water covering the surface would fill no more than a teacup. A third of the Earth's water is sweet water, three-quarters of which are frozen solid in the Antarctic. The numbers of species living in water vastly exceeds those living on land. It is estimated that 90 percent of all organisms live in the oceans.

Water has one wonderfully anomalous characteristic that is crucial to life on Earth. When it freezes, water increases in volume with the result that it can float in its own element—in keeping with the Archimedean principle which states that a body immersed in a fluid is buoyed up by a force equal to the weight of the displaced fluid. If this were not so, the oceans would progressively ice over. Water can also climb. By means of the attraction of molecule to molecule through capillary forces, the life-giving fluid rises upwards in plants and trees passing from the roots to the crown, up to eighty meters above the ground. In addition, water stores huge quantities of energy in the form of warmth, transporting it along ocean currents, such as the Gulf Stream in the Northern Hemisphere, thereby softening the climate along the east coast of North America and in northern and western Europe.

The sea was the first dumping ground used by human beings and, despite environmental conferences, it has become the largest deposit not only for huge amounts of rubbish but also for chemical toxins. Jacques Cousteau, the pioneering environmentalist, talked of a "rotting paradise" as he railed against the yearly pollution of the world's oceans with millions of tons of chemical waste from the industrialized world, waste that includes mercury, cadmium, and lead. While river water can reach a biological "tipping point" at which underwater flora and fauna start to die off, up until now—by virtue of a complex system of self-cleansing currents—the oceans have always been able to regenerate themselves. But what happens when an ocean reaches its tipping point?

Water is a source of nutrition that is not present in limitless quantities, even in rainy regions. Rainwater is by no means as precious as drinking water. In the natural cycle, rainwater only gradually turns into drinking water by being filtered through different strata of rock. Drinking water has to be odorless and colorless, it must contain a minimum of minerals, and have a pH value between 6.5 and 8.5. A human being needs only two to three liters daily in order to survive; nevertheless, the overall water consumption per inhabitant in industrialized societies ranges between 120 and 180 liters per day. By far the greater part of that is consumed washing, and flushing the toilet.

Seventy percent of the human body is made up of water containing traces of salt. "The salt content of our bodies alone," to quote Jacques Cousteau, "is a sign of what we have inherited from the sea, of our kinship with the creatures who first rose up out of the waters of the oceans" (*The Cousteau Almanac: An Inventory of Life on our Water Planet* [Garden City, N.Y.: Doubleday, 1981] Vol. 6). And in his poem, "Song of the Spirits over the Waters," Johann Wolfgang von Goethe compares the cycle of the element water with that of the life of human beings: "The Soul of

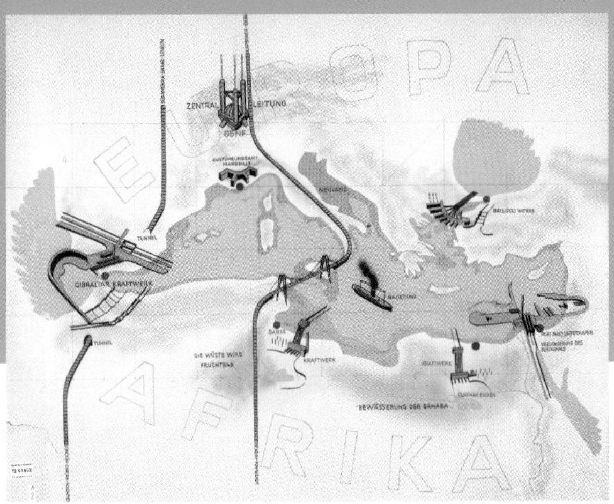

Map of the utopian Atlantropa, a project by the Munich architect Herman Sörgel, 1928–52

"The World" is a ship that carries luxury vacation homes to the four corners of the Earth.

man, /It is like water: /It comes from heaven, /And earthward again /Descends /Eternally changing" (*Goethe, The Collected Works, Vol. 1: Selected Poems* [Princeton: Princeton University Press, 1994], 71).

Myths

As one of the four elements, water—and its symbolism—has played a central role in the mythology, religion and rituals of all cultures. These myths seem to emerge from a dream world and are associated with wisdom and the subconscious.

Creation stories in particular have generated a wealth of related myths. In Indian mythology, Vishnu descends into the water and raises up the Earth. In Greek tales of the gods, the sea, Pontos, is born at the same time as the heavens, Uranos, from the womb of the Earth goddess, Gaia. A legend from Papua New Guinea tells of the primeval waters that covered the Earth with just one creature swimming in them—a giant turtle which, searching for a place to rest, heaped up sand which in turn became inhabitable land. This mythological image reappears in the children's book *Jäpkes Insel* [Jäpke's Island] by Lenore Gaul, in which the hero of the story rests on an island which is in reality the back of a turtle.

In the myths surrounding the beginnings of the planet Earth, there are repeated descriptions of the destruction of life by a catastrophic flood. This seems to be a reflection of a traumatic experience shared by many human beings. Even the Sumerian-Babylonian Gilgamesh epic, the oldest poem known to us today, describes a devastating flood. As a counterbalance to the flood we find the primal image of survival on water in the form of the Ark of the Old Testament, a floating box (the Latin for box is *arca*), which Noah exactingly constructed according to God's instructions, with the result that he, his family, and representatives of the animal kingdom survived the forty-day flood. In the Book of Genesis, the Lord speaks to Noah telling him, "Make yourself an ark of gopher wood; make rooms in the ark, and cover it inside and out with pitch. This is how you are to make it: the length of the ark three hundred cubits, its breadth fifty cubits, and its height thirty cubits" (Gen. 6:14–15 RSV). Assuming that a cubit is 44.5 centimeters, this would mean that in our own terms the arch was 133.5 meters long, just under 22.3 meters wide and 13.4 meters high. These are huge dimensions, unheard of in any other records about ancient vessels; in fact they are equivalent to those of a medium-sized freight ship today.

Our fears of another such flood have surprisingly come back to life through the warnings from scientists of the consequences of global warming. The various forms that a potential apocalypse might take are simulated in computer programs, and spectacularly envisioned in genre films like *The Day After Tomorrow* (2004), directed by Roland Emmerich. Kevin Costner's *Waterworld* (1995) went a step further with its representation of life in a distant future when water covers the whole Earth and memories of civilizations on dry land are dismissed as fairytales. The survivors build primitive floating islands from flotsam left behind by the great catastrophe. The people live as water nomads and adapt to their new habitat,

Stone Age village on stilts on Lake Constance, Unteruhldingen, Germany

Palazzi on the Grand Canal in Venice, Italy

developing webbed feet and gills through mutation. The future seems to be a replay of the past.

Narcissus fell in love with his mirror image when he glimpsed it in a well. This same capacity of water to reflect light and to mirror existing phenomena led to the popular notion that there is a parallel world beneath the surface of the water, which imitates life on land. In the story of little Tom in Charles Kingsley's *The Water-Babies* we read: "Are there not water-rats, water-flies, water-crickets, water-crabs, water-tortoises, water-scorpions, water-tigers and water-hodges…—then why not water-babies?" (*The Water-Babies* [London, 1958], 61). The world of water myths is starkly divided into Good and Evil—sea monsters, rays, and giant squids on one hand; undines, mermaids, water nymphs, and other semi-human water creatures on the other. The latter inhabit an ephemeral world; they appear only fleetingly yet they play an important part in folklore all over the world. With their magical beauty and siren songs the daughters of the sea king lure sailors into the waves or help the shipwrecked reach shore. Famous nymphs from antiquity, such as Galathea, live on in the names of ships and research projects (page 100). But friendships between humans and water nymphs often come to a tragic end. Hans Christian Andersen's Little Mermaid never wins the full love of her Prince and in the end is transformed into sea foam.

Conflicts

For centuries, human beings have felt threatened by the sea. A calm sea is never to be trusted and it seems that storms and floods reveal the true character of this unpredictable element. Reclaiming land from the sea has always been one of the great dreams of humankind. Even the restless Faust considers, shortly before his death in the second part of Goethe's tragedy, whether he could redeem his misdemeanors by setting in motion gigantic schemes to reclaim land for his fellow human beings: "Grasp then the priceless triumph, evermore / To hold the lordly ocean from the shore, / To set the watery waste new boundary lines, / And bid it wallow in its own confines" (*Faust, Part 2* [New York: Penguin Classic, 1960], Act IV).

It was in the 20th century that the first large-scale land reclamation projects were realized, completely changing the geography of some countries. In the Netherlands, the late 1920s saw the Zuider Zee project, separating the IJsselmeer from the North Sea and creating polders to be used for agriculture and the construction of new towns. The mania for technical progress reached a bizarre climax in the utopian Atlantropa by the Munich architect Herman Sörgel. According to his plans, a mighty dam in the Straits of Gibraltar would lower the water level in the Mediterranean by two hundred meters. His idea was that Europe and Africa should become one continent called Atlantropa, supplied with energy from gigantic power stations in the shape of dams placed at the inlets of the Mediterranean. Renowned architects contributed designs to this project. Erich Mendelsohn took on a

West Pier in Brighton, England

Hotel houseboats in Srinagar, Kashmir

leading role in the organization and Peter Behrens—teacher of Bauhaus founder Walter Gropius—devised a lock for Gibraltar with a four hundred-meter tower, taller than any other building at that time.

Since the mid-20th century there has been a counter-movement, no longer concerned with reclaiming land. Instead, an awareness of the rapid increase in the world's population has led to the discovery of the seas as a possible future home for human beings, and ideas for living and working on water are being developed. The pioneers who paved the way for this approach include Jacques Cousteau, Kyonori Kikutake, Kenzo Tange, and Richard Buckminster Fuller.

In the 1950s, when the space race was just beginning, Fuller suggested that the solution for the immediate problems of humankind lay not in outer space but in the Earth's oceans. Japan, with its critical density of human beings and industrial sites, became the center for the new thinking. According to the ideas of the Metabolists, a group of young architects working in Tokyo in the early 1960s, people could live and work on water and visit dry land just for relaxation. Kenzo Tange proposed a superstructure above Tokyo Bay running along a linear, "communal axis" which would take into account the crucial importance to society of mobility. The first project realized for a town on water was designed by Kikutake for the 1975 International Ocean Exposition in Okinawa (page 92), but it was broken up again after just twenty-five years. Despite this failure, many are now working with an "expanded" concept of architecture which no longer restricts construction projects to dry land alone—witness the water towns in the Netherlands which leave the water's edge untouched. Areas of wetland, once regarded as ugly and unhealthy, are now appreciated as valuable landscapes. In some places the polders are even being returned to their natural state (page 28).

In reality, the floating city where people choose a dwelling on water rather than purchasing a house already exists. The city is called *The World*, and is to date the world's only oceanic, residential scheme. Actually, the residences are only in the temporary ownership of their occupants, because these one hundred to three hundred-square-meter homes are leased for just fifty years—the projected lifetime of the ship itself. The occupants of *The World* are generally the erstwhile owners of ocean-going yachts who no longer want to be bothered with running their maritime holiday homes. The ship-city slowly and steadily circumnavigates the world. The greatest luxury on board: as much time as you like.

History

The history of human beings living on water goes back to prehistoric times. Their floating or fixed habitations generally took one of three main forms: pile dwellings, rafts, or ships. These three ancient types of water architecture are still with us today.

The earliest structures built by human beings in water use stilts. As excavations have shown—particularly in Switzerland and at Lake Constance—in the Neolithic Period, around 7,000 years ago, there were already settlements on water. In Unteruhldingen, Germany, on Lake Constance, the findings from archaeological

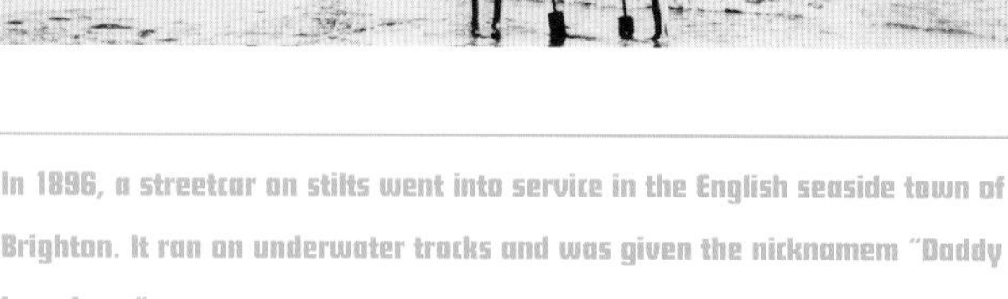

In 1896, a streetcar on stilts went into service in the English seaside town of Brighton. It ran on underwater tracks and was given the nicknamem "Daddy Long-legs."

Illustration of Captain Nemo's Nautilus from Jules Verne's "20,000 Leagues Under the Sea"

excavations have made it possible to reconstruct a whole village on stilts from around 4000 BC, including household items and tools. Buildings on stilts offered natural protection against predatory animals and hostile neighbors; even floods could not harm them. In addition, living on water was healthier than living in marshlands. In Southeast Asia and New Guinea, the tradition of living in houses on stilts has survived over the millennia into our own time. In Europe, whole cities—Amsterdam, St. Petersburg, and Venice—were built on piles driven into the sea bed. Architects today still turn to this form of construction, using industrial materials like aluminum (page 26). We still see the principle of structures on stilts in its original form in the piers leading out to sea from beach promenades. Piers are like fragments of bridges jutting out into the water. With the constant wind, the rhythmic lapping of the waves against the wooden posts, and the view of an endless horizon, anyone out for a stroll along a pier cannot help but feel at one with the sea.

The oldest floating structures were built on rafts and were developed considerably later than the first pile dwellings. Sumerian cuneiform texts from the height of Mesopotamian civilization tell of floating villages 5,000 years ago on the Euphrates and the Tigris. These early structures were built entirely from reeds—both the rafts and the edifices on them. Situated in reed beds on the shores of the rivers, these villages—home to the marsh Arabs—were shielded from the gaze of those who lived on dry land because they so perfectly blended into their surroundings. The camouflage was so effective that certain village communities survived into the 20th century, unnoticed by Western researchers and unaffected by the progress of our technological civilization.

In Europe, the concept of the raft was largely influenced by the annual flow of newly felled tree trunks downriver. During these journeys, which could take several months, workers lived in primitive huts on a raft of tree trunks. It was an immensely dangerous life, fraught with many privations. Rafts were not only difficult to navigate, they sometimes broke into pieces again.

In 1947, the Norwegian anthropologist Thor Heyerdahl crossed the Pacific Ocean on his balsa wood raft, Kon-Tiki, in a bid to prove that Polynesia was settled by peoples from South America. The success of his expedition was greeted with great enthusiasm, especially amongst the young, and Kon-Tiki became a symbol for autarkic adventures on the high seas.

Modern water houses built on pontoons, as in the case of Herman Hertzberger's Watervilla (page 56) and the Spaceframe project by N55 (page 52), recall practice of constructing dwellings on top of rafts.

Conventional houseboats with a ship's hull also have a tradition going back thousands of years and are an integral part of numerous major cities in China, India, Thailand, Cambodia, and Vietnam. The houseboats in these regions serve not only as dwellings but also lodge workshops and commercial units of every kind. There are weekly markets that only differ from markets on dry land in that the farmers travel to the city by boat and offer their products for sale directly from the water. Whole urban districts consist of houseboats, connected to each other by a labyrinthine network of

Underwater fortress from the James Bond movie "The Spy Who Loved Me," 1977

Futurama undersea city at the New York World's Fair of 1964

waterways. These are full-fledged water towns that—just like the towns on terra firma—are often bursting at the seams. Nevertheless, they still give their residents a feeling of independence, each on his or her own little "island." People come from far and wide to see the houseboats in Srinagar, Kashmir. Intricately carved palaces made from long-lasting teak bob on the water. At night, when thousands of lights reflect on Lake Dal, the town takes on the magical glow that can only come from a community living on water.

In North America, settlements on water developed for very different reasons. The first water communities grew up in the wake of the logging activities along the great rivers of Canada. At first, the rafts had only simple huts where the workers could sleep. In time, these primitive beginnings developed into floating villages with houseboats for whole families, kitchens, floating hotels, and other small businesses. Some of these water communities exist until today (page 68). In Seattle, settlements grew up on water to meet the needs of the maritime workers, providing accommodation close to where they worked. During the Second World War, seventy-five thousand workers flocked to San Francisco Bay and lived in prefabricated houses, working in the docks, building Liberty ships to transport cargo during the war. After the war ingenious workers constructed houseboats from debris material. Many of these veteran houseboats have been carefully preserved today and can be admired in Marin County. In contrast to the workers' homes, there are rather different houseboats in Sausalito Bay near San Francisco. As far back as the 19th century, wealthy citizens used to spend the summer in this "leisure park" with its cultural events and fireworks. Nowadays these houseboats are occupied by an idealistic community of latter-day hippies.

In Europe, the tradition of houseboats in permanent moorings has survived, particularly along the canals and inland waterways of France and the Netherlands. A canal fringed by houseboats on either side is a familiar part of the cityscape in Amsterdam and Paris. Houseboats convey a sense of protection and seem to offer a life untouched by the hectic pace of the big city, possessing its own rules. Defunct barges are lovingly restored by architects and converted into loftboats (pages 48–51). Nevertheless, in many European cities those living in houseboats are subject to considerable restrictions. It seems that a highly evolved feeling of permanence and order on dry land actively resists the notion of life on houseboats. It is only now, in the 21st century, that municipal authorities are discovering houseboats and water homes as ecologically viable alternatives to building on dry land. Taking the Netherlands as their model, German cities such as Hamburg and Berlin are now promoting schemes for living on the water, offering a lifestyle that is close to nature without choking up the shoreline (pages 58–61).

With the construction of underwater living quarters, initially for deep-sea exploration, the history of living in water took on a whole new dimension. Many projects concerned with underwater living are still purely utopian, inspired by Jules Verne's descriptions of the adventures of Captain Nemo and his vessel, the *Nautilus*. The *Nautilus* was not so much a submarine as a small, self-sufficient underwater community which derived its energy from salt water.

Jean Nouvel's "Monolith" at the Expo.02 in Switzerland

Bathing machines in Ostende, Belgium

In James Bond movies, the underwater world has long been a firm fixture. Unobserved, evil individuals like Dr. Stromberg in *The Spy Who Loved Me* control their empires from luxurious underwater fortresses. In the 1960s, the euphoric desire to explore the oceans—just as space was being conquered—reached a high point. At the New York World's Fair of 1964, visions of the colonization of space and the oceans were presented as *Futurama*. These visions of the future were not just the product of a pioneering spirit, but were intended above all to offer a response to the ever-increasing global population. Projections of the rate of population growth have proved to be correct, but so far the resulting problems have only been addressed with conventional methods.

Aesthetics

This book focuses on the adaption of architecture to water, but there are also examples where water has been integrated into the architecture itself as a design feature. Here, too, there are traditions reaching into the distant past, which are shaped not least by different cultural responses to water, be they based on fear or affection. In Europe, the relationship to water is colored by natural philosophy and alchemy. In Asia, aside from the symbolic cleansing power of water, the relationship is defined by aesthetics. This led to the construction of temples that create a symbolic balance between water and architecture, which is in turn used as a basis for meditation.

In Europe, it was particularly the bucolic age of the Baroque that produced a wealth of fantastic water architecture with artfully sweeping lakes and intricate water features. These served not only as a focus for meditation but also as the backdrop for events designed to entertain the people, sometimes with specially composed music such as Georg Friedrich Handel's *Water Music*. In the 19th century, a rigidly moralistic, bourgeois epoch set in, which looked askance at the pleasures of the senses: a time that could produce a curiosity such as the bathing machine. With the sexes strictly segregated, those wishing to bathe would rent a bathing machine in which they could change and be towed out to sea, usually by horses. At that point the bather would descend into the water from his or her little domicile, protected as much as possible from unseemly observation. As bathing morals relaxed, the bathing machine disappeared from view again.

Not unrelated to the concept of this book is the residential home, Falling Water, designed by the American architect Frank Lloyd Wright and built in 1937 above a tumultuous waterfall in Bear Run, Pennsylvania. Such close proximity to water creates a distinct quality of life, underpinned by symbolic and aesthetic associations, which recall the characteristics of Japanese architecture. Falling Water is admired as a revolutionary concept which opened up a huge potential for the future.

The French architect Jean Nouvel forayed into a rather more abstract aesthetic dimension with his contribution to *Expo.02* in Switzerland. He placed a massive steel cube—measuring thirty-four meters cubed and clad in iron plates—in a lake in Murten. This structure is an example of the transition from architectural forms to purely geometric sculpture; built vertical

Lighthouse in Four, Brittany, France

New design for Brighton's West Pier by Foreign Office Architects

planes are confronted by and confront the natural horizontal surface of the water.

The meeting point between functional architecture and aesthetically defined landmarks has to be the lighthouse, which marks the boundary between land and sea and is often exposed to the crashing waves. Originally a functional tower, by now it has become more of a symbolic structure which, in every civilization, stands for shelter and safety.

Towards the end of the 20th century, water—as a design aspect in construction—seemed to come to the fore again. As a forum for technological innovation and architectural experiment, the Architecture Biennale of 2004 in Venice presented proposals for urban expansion as *The Metamorphosis of the Cities on Water*. Realized projects, such as the reclamation of abandoned airfields along the coast near Athens for sports venues and a marina, and the development of the waterfront in Barcelona, clearly show that not only architects but also town planners are incorporating water, as a new living space, into their plans for the future.

Concept

This book is the fruit of a long-lasting love of the subject. Both authors have spent many years living by lakes or the sea, in daily contact with the water and the people who venture onto and into it, and who live nearby it.

This book presents the possibilities of water as a viable living space in four categories—Standing Tall, Floating Homes, Submerging Architecture, and Frozen Hard. Selected projects reveal the immense range of the fascinating world of water architecture and the technologies involved, as well as the multiplicity of questions these raise and the solutions that have been suggested. The wealth of ideas coming from architects, designers, artists, and visionaries as well as the examples of vernacular architecture will surely inspire hydrophile readers to new creative heights of their own.

Christian Burchard, Felix Flesche

Tall buildings, embodying the most daring of engineering concepts, rise over one thousand meters out of the water. Artificial archipelagos become miniature worlds while massive drilling platforms make the Eiffel Tower look rather small and fragile. The first part of this book presents structures that stand above the water on some stable construction—stilts and piles of all kinds—and artificial islands that rise out of the water. All these structures, firmly attached to the ground below them, easily resist the movement of the water. An interesting feature of this section is the concept of amphibious living in areas prone to flooding, such as Holland. Town planners are increasingly attempting to make peace with the water, no longer reclaiming land by constructing higher dykes and sand embankments. The construction of "amphibious" homes means that precious coastal areas can be preserved.
In addition to this, artificial islands—intensively exploited in some areas—make it possible to considerably increase the number of properties along the shoreline and to extend beaches.

Standing Tall

1234

Troll A Offshore Gas Production Platform

Eighty Kilometers Northwest of Bergen, Norway, 1991–1995

Some time in the distant future, when archaeologists are poring over the remnants of our civilization, they will find evidence of huge, mysterious structures in the oceans, bigger and more solid than anything on land. Perhaps these structures will become the source of myth and legend about our own times. Even for us, the visual generation, these titans that have taken the modern maxim of "form follows function" to awe-inspiring dimensions almost defy imagination.

The 300-meter-high Eiffel Tower in Paris seems small and fragile in comparison to the four massive concrete towers of the 451-meter-high Norwegian Troll A production platform. The actual platform stands more than a hundred meters above the surface of the water and is designed to withstand twenty-five-meter waves. Another sensational feature of this structure is its mobility. The towers were built in a coastal dry dock and towed out to sea by tugs, eighty kilometers northwest of Bergen. More than 160 people live on the rig, working around the clock in shifts to bring gas to the surface from a depth of fifteen hundred meters. The gas is channeled through underwater pipelines to Emden in Germany and Zeebrugge in Belgium. Current calculations project that the Norwegian Shelf will be able to provide 10 percent of Western Europe's gas for several generations.

There are 420 drilling platforms in the North Sea alone. Most of them are steel structures covering an area the size of a football field. Whereas gas resources are likely to remain viable for a considerable period of time, experts reckon oil supplies will have run out by the year 2030. Until that time, there are also floating platforms capable of drilling for oil at depths of more than two thousand meters.

In a study of offshore drilling platforms from the point of view of cultural history, François Béguin, professor of human sciences at the Versailles School of Architecture, has described their construction as an archaic struggle between technology and nature: "Transported far out into the upper latitudes of the North Sea, the instrumental violence of the platform can only freight the obligatory resistance that man must oppose to the violence of the elements."

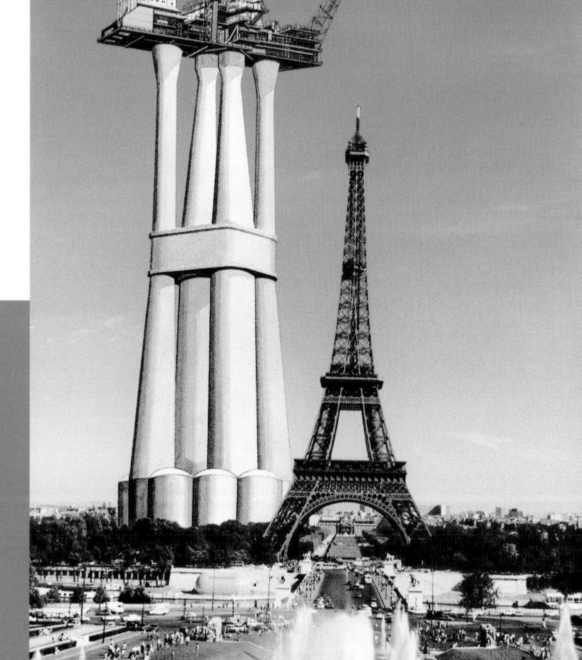

Eberhard Zeidler

Ontario Place, Toronto, Canada, 1968–1971

In the 1950s and 60s, the construction of city highways challenged the organically developed structure of many industrial cities. In Toronto, vast swathes of transport infrastructure separated the city from the shores of Lake Ontario. Canadian architect Eberhard Zeidler, a German immigrant, began to regain the shoreline for the people of Toronto with his urban park, the Ontario Place project, creating an artificial peninsula with a yachting marina and five exhibition pavilions in the sheltered bay. The light and open development seems so modern and cutting edge that tourists visiting Ontario Place today are often astonished to find that it was built in the 1960s.

This is no purist, abstract architecture, as a first glance at the plans might suggest, but a charmingly whimsical approach to complex forms and technology high above the waterline. The stringently orthogonal grid layout with its simple geometric elements sets a counterpoint to the organic forms of the harbor. The three-story pavilions hang from four central pylons, in the manner of a suspension bridge, with wire-hung trusses for structural stability. The facade of white-coated steel and glass conceals a skeleton frame on a cruciform basis with protruding corners and intersections for connecting bridges.

In the evening light, the Ontario Place skyline is reflected in the water. The silhouettes of the high pylons with their cables recall the masts of ships becalmed, echoing the yachts in the harbor. There could be no clearer illustration of Zeidler's success in achieving his aim of "the meeting of water and land brought to a poetic awareness," as he noted on one of his first sketches for the project. This idealistic notion of lyrically merging architecture and landscape was one that was hotly debated at the time. Critics, very much in the spirit of the 1960s, called for more investment in "nature" than in "architecture."

Ontario Place is a continuation of the lightweight structures pioneered by Richard Buckminster Fuller and Frei Otto. The three-story pavilions are supported by pylons with wire-hung trusses in the manner of a suspension bridge. Built in the 1960s to a design by Canadian architect Eberhard Zeidler, this project still looks innovatively modern.

MVRDV

Silodam, Amsterdam, The Netherlands, 1995–2002

"For us, architecture is just an everyday thing, almost as popular as football," says one representative of the architectural centers that offer planning and design advice in many Dutch communities. This helps to explain the experimental, even radical, and highly unconventional architecture that thrives in the Netherlands. Indeed, these days, tourists flock to this tiny country as much for its modern architecture as for its charming canals and Old Masters.

Among the country's internationally renowned buildings are the innovative and controversial projects designed by the Rotterdam team of architects, Winy Maas, Jacob van Rijs, and Nathalie de Vries. Silodam, a 300-meter-long residential complex in the western port area of Amsterdam is one example of MVRDV's exacting architectural standards.

The long, colorful building floats like a huge cargo ship on a matrix of concrete piers in the River Ij. It provides homes for a broad social mix, from privately owned luxury apartments with their own inner court-yards to low-income public housing, as well as artists' studios and commercial premises. The rooms are staggered in the vertical, horizontal, and diagonal so that the number of floors in each unit differs.

The design is a carefully orchestrated architectural system based on sociological studies. Grouping four to eight apartments in "mini-city districts" with their own elevator and their own distinctive color scheme fosters a sense of community. Color is also used on the exterior to delineate the various parts of the building and emphasize the different story heights.

Needless to say, there are also meeting places where urban life and suburban life overlap. At water level, there is a panorama terrace and a restaurant, as well as small marinas and moorings for boats. The residents also have access to promenades and public balconies throughout the building.

The choice of facade material could hardly have been more varied, or more at odds with conventional design rules. Brick alternates with metal, glass, and wood—low-cost materials that counter the heaviness of the building while at the same time giving it an air of improvisation. The architects consciously created this effect because the building is intended to be neither elitist nor permanent. The uninterrupted views of Amsterdam and the River Ij—with its bustling shipping traffic—are breathtaking.

The Silodam apartment complex by MVRDV in Amsterdam is the result of painstaking analysis of urban planning and housing construction. A complex spatial system provides for maisonette apartments. Several units are grouped together in "villages." This social and spatial structure is also reflected in the patchwork facade.

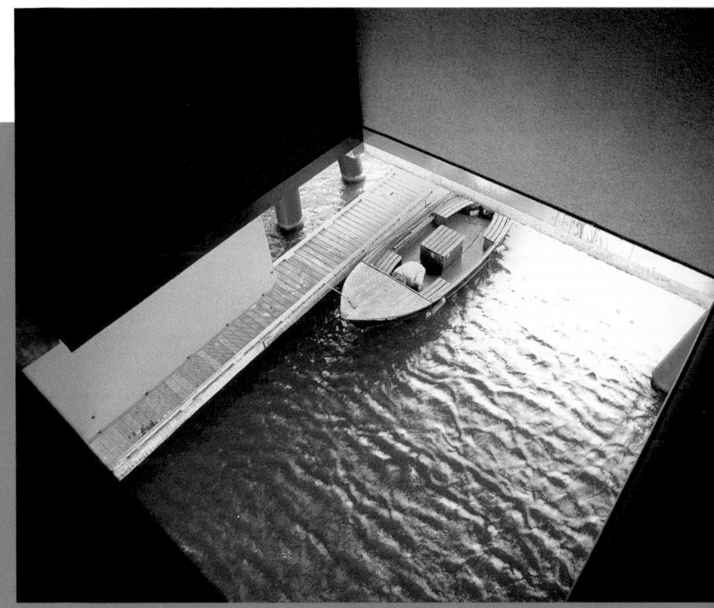

Micha de Haas

Aluminium Forest, Houten, The Netherlands, 1997–2001

"The Aluminium Center crowns
The treetops of the aluminium woodland,
Above slender stems through which the flickering Dutch light filters, falters
And reflects." (From a poem by Micha de Haas about Aluminium Forest)

The magical, shimmering aluminum complex by Dutch architect Micha de Haas—on the shores of a lake in Houten near Utrecht—looks like a minimalist tree house. This postmodernist building on stilts seems almost improvised as the aluminum rods, on which the block of the building appears to hover weightlessly, are of differing diameters and some tilted at varying angles. It is this "undergrowth" of aluminum rods from which the building takes its name of Aluminium Forest.

The building, built entirely of aluminum, is a showcase and promotional center for the Dutch aluminum industry's umbrella organization. The filigree substructure of 368 aluminum tubes stands in a bed of crushed bauxite, the mineral that provides the raw material for this lightweight metal. The six-meter-high tubes not only have a load-bearing function, but also house the plumbing and sewage systems, the electrical cabling, and the heating pump. Inside the building, the offices and exhibition areas are grouped around atrium spaces that emphasize the transparency and lightness of the structure. The entrance is accessed by elevator or by stairway ramps. When the building is not in use, the ramps can be pulled up like drawbridges, making the structure an impregnable stronghold.

A number of innovative techniques have been developed and tested for this building. The trusses of the roof frame are not bolted together but linked by a sleeve system used in modern aviation manufacture. The extraordinary precision of the extruder profiles used here allowed quick and simple installation of the windows and interior fittings. In theory, at least, the building could easily be dismantled and moved to another site; or if demolished the elements of the building can be entirely recycled—an impressive ecological achievement.

With Aluminium Forest, the Amsterdam-based architect Micha de Haas has succeeded in creating a high-tech structure of enormous symbolic significance for the industry using formal methods of trans-high tech. This sensational building was awarded the Special Prize of the Architecture and Technology Award 2003.

The promotional center designed by Amsterdam-based architect Micha de Haas stands on a "forest" of 368 aluminum tubes. It is both innovatively high-tech and lyrically evocative, its shining aluminum rods recalling Holland's poplars. In high winds, the rods vibrate and "sing."

Klunder Architecten

Plan Tij, Dordrecht, The Netherlands, Project, 2004

For centuries, water was Holland's public enemy number one. And for generations, the Dutch struggled to reclaim land; building polders and securing them with dykes to prevent flooding. In the course of time, a man-made landscape was created, crisscrossed by canals and locks and bridges. In recent years, there has been a radical change in attitudes to water in the Netherlands, where it is now welcomed as an enrichment of the urban environment. Suburbs and housing estates are planned along the waterfront and even in the water. In some places, polders are even being turned back into lakes.

Plan Tij—Dutch for ebb and flow—by the Rotterdam-based architects Rien de Ruiter and Sjoerd Berghuis is one of a new generation of "wet-footed" architectural developments that is deliberately geared towards the water. Plan Tij comprises a range of different types of buildings. The box-like houses along the former riverbanks near Dordrecht are raised on pylons, some in the form of a row of compact terraced housing jutting into the open water like a jetty, others scattered among the reeds on the shore. The natural environment remains unaltered. Instead of front gardens, the houses have spacious patios set back within the building to shelter them from the wind.

Plan Tij is remarkable not only for its sensitive approach to the water zones, but also for its unusual urban planning concept which does not place the new housing areas as separate developments on the outskirts of town, but integrates them into the landscape. The houses form demarcation lines in the flat plains of the polders and create charming landmarks rather like copses of trees.

The Plan Tij concept is part of a new architectural movement in the Netherlands that works with the water instead of against it. The cuboid housing blocks are set on stilts high enough above the water to require no additional flood protection.

Hoogstad Architecten, DHV AIB, D3BN, and Droog Design

Hybrid-Highrise, No Fixed Location, Project, 2002

Since the oil crisis of 1973 and subsequent American surveys on the limits of growth, fossil fuel conservation and project sustainability have become existential problems in the industrialized world. In the Netherlands, an interdisciplinary team of architects, scientists, engineers, and designers has developed a far-sighted model for high-rise buildings: the Hybrid-Highrise.

The name Hybrid refers to the combination of offshore structural techniques and the exploitation of greenhouse effects in drastically reducing energy consumption. Using the so-called *serre* concept (French for greenhouse) the entire high-rise tower is clad in a transparent textile or glass. This generates a microclimate inside that resembles a vast wintergarden and allows for large areas of greenery and all-weather public space. Moreover, the conical membrane structure of the building complex has a futuristic look in which the building mass seems to dissolve into translucency.

The Hybrid-Highrise has a steel skeleton construction consisting of prefabricated components into which the floors are slotted. These modular elements of the load-bearing frame, which can be assembled by robot-controlled production processes, provide considerable flexibility in the vertical and horizontal design. Because of the sophisticated modular technique, changes to the floorplan can even be made during construction. If the building is demolished, the steel structure can be dismantled and reassembled elsewhere, or simply recycled.

A team of Dutch architects and designers has come up with an urban high-rise concept that can be built in coastal waters using offshore technology. Constructing the tower as a kind of greenhouse has several advantages: low energy consumption, high standards of comfort, and innovative aesthetics.

Maria Rosa Cervera, Javier Pioz, and Eloy Celaya

Bionic Tower, Shanghai, China, Project, Since 1996

How can a branch withstand the force of the wind? How can a lightweight tubular bone carry hundredweight loads? These are questions of bionics, an innovative science that studies the systematic structures and processes of nature that have evolved over millions of years. The applications of bionics range from improving the aerodynamics of aircraft to creating water-resistant surfaces, and even includes miniature hydraulics based on the leg movements of spiders. In the field of civil engineering and architecture, however, bionics is still a relative newcomer. Now, the Spanish architects Maria Rosa Cervera, Javier Pioz, and Eloy Celaya have used bionics to help them design a skyscraper more than 1.2 kilometers high that can house some 100,000 people.

Conventional skyscrapers can rise to a maximum height of about 700 meters. In order to break through this ceiling, the Madrid-based team of architects experimented with biological structures and their application in structural and civil engineering. The result of their findings is a truly titanic high-rise; its streamlined contours soaring to the heavens. Their first studies were undertaken in 1999 for the realization of the project in Hong Kong, but for geological reasons a new site had to be found and recent plans have concentrated on the densely populated Shanghai region.

The tower design has three hundred floors—twelve blocks of twenty-five stories each form partial cities with their own green areas, hotels, and shopping levels. At its widest, the circular building is 196 meters in diameter and the foundation extends 200 meters underground. The tower is set in the middle of an artificial lake one kilometer in diameter, designed to buffer shock waves in case of an earthquake. On the shores of the artificial lake there will be a business center with lower skyscrapers and a separate infrastructure. According to initial estimates, the complex will take fifteen years to build.

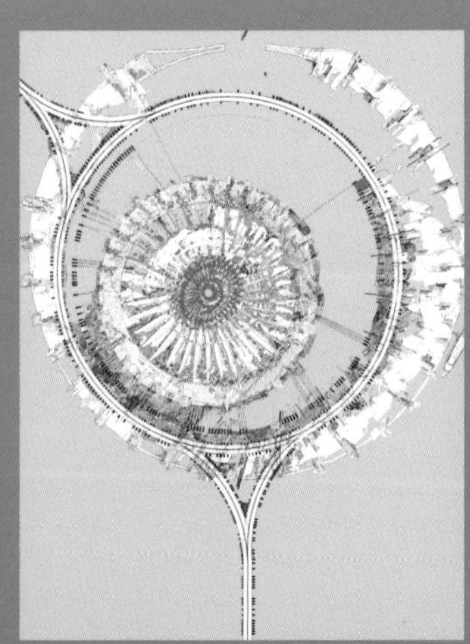

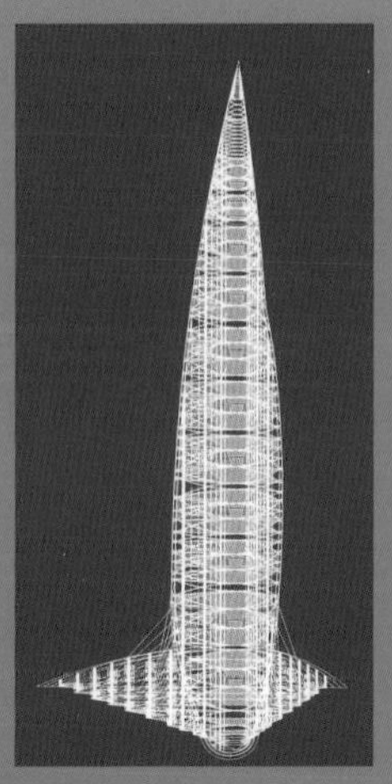

At present, the world's highest building is Taipei 0101 in Taipei, Taiwan, at 508 meters, followed by the Petronas Towers in Kuala Lumpur. Skyscrapers have withstood all natural catastrophes to date and lasted as much as three generations. Although the high-rise dream was muted by the events of September 11, 2001, it was not abandoned. Spanish architects Cervera, Pioz, and Celaya envision a Bionic Tower more than a kilometer high; where as many as 100,000 people will live and work, leaving the tower only for holidays.

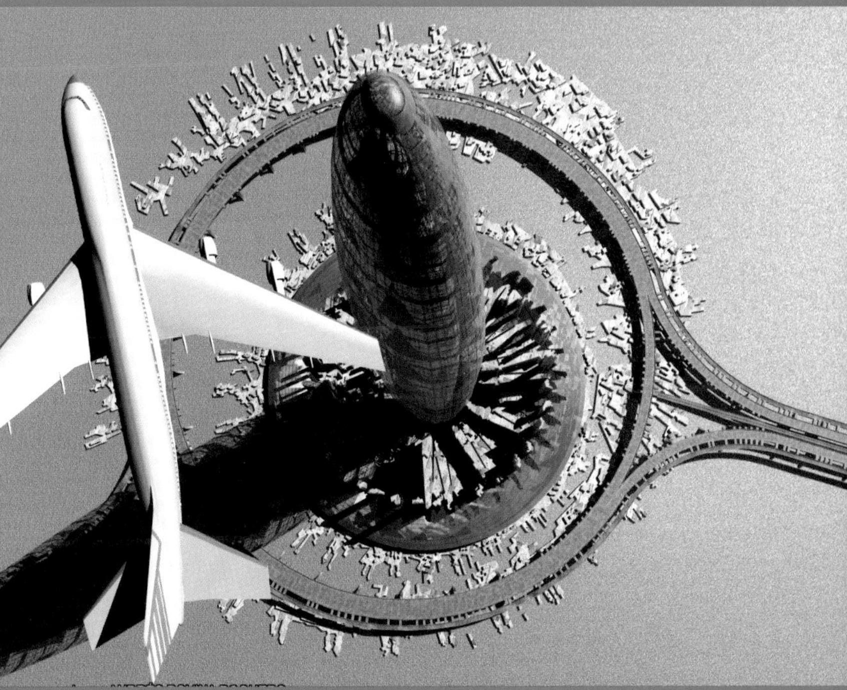

Meinhard von Gerkan (von Gerkan, Marg und Partner)

Luchao Harbour City, Shanghai, China, 2002–2005

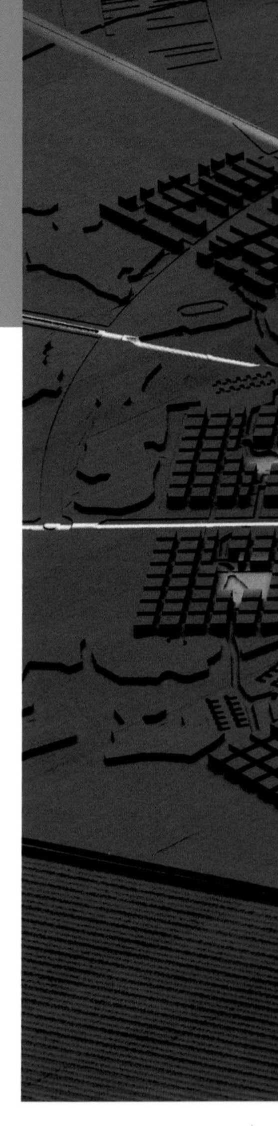

Since the dawn of urban culture, humankind has been fascinated by the notion of the ideal city. In ancient times, this took the form of a city with temples and palaces at its center, mirroring in its aesthetic perfection and harmony the religious worldview of the prevailing civilization. Within the defensive walls of the city, people lived in districts corresponding to a strict, hierarchical social structure. The ideal city was designed on the drawing board: the most common layout being either rectangular or circular forms. This principle can be seen in the square arrangement of saintly Jerusalem and in Plato's vision of the ideal city as concentric circles.

In Chinese, *luchao* means "born of a droplet." This poetic term is the name and concept for an ideal city of the 21st century built on an artificially extended peninsula fifty kilometers southwest of Shanghai. The Hamburg firm of architects used the image of the concentric waves created when a drop falls on a water surface as their metaphorical basis for this urban project—the biggest of its kind in the world—designed to accommodate some 300,000 inhabitants. The heart of the city is the lake at the center in which there will be islands with museums, theaters, and concert halls.

The city is made up of three circular zones. Around the lakeshore promenade is a dense service infrastructure or business district with offices, shopping malls, pedestrian zones, and some apartment blocks. The second ring is a broad green belt with libraries, multipurpose halls, and cultural facilities. On the periphery are residential districts—arranged in a checkerboard layout—each accommodating up to 13,000 people. Each section is grouped around a lake, reiterating the overall concept on a smaller scale. Ring-shaped and radial waterways link and separate the individual districts and give the city its distinctive character: schools, athletic fields, a university, and an airport are loosely scattered around the city as points of orientation. The initial construction phase for 80,000 inhabitants is scheduled for completion by 2005; the second and third phases are to be completed by 2020.

In the inland lake, at the precise intersection of the urban axial lines, a filigree structure rises towards the heavens. Halfway up, water jets produce an artificial mist that condenses in a cloud. This "cloud needle" symbolizes the city's mythical origins in a droplet of water.

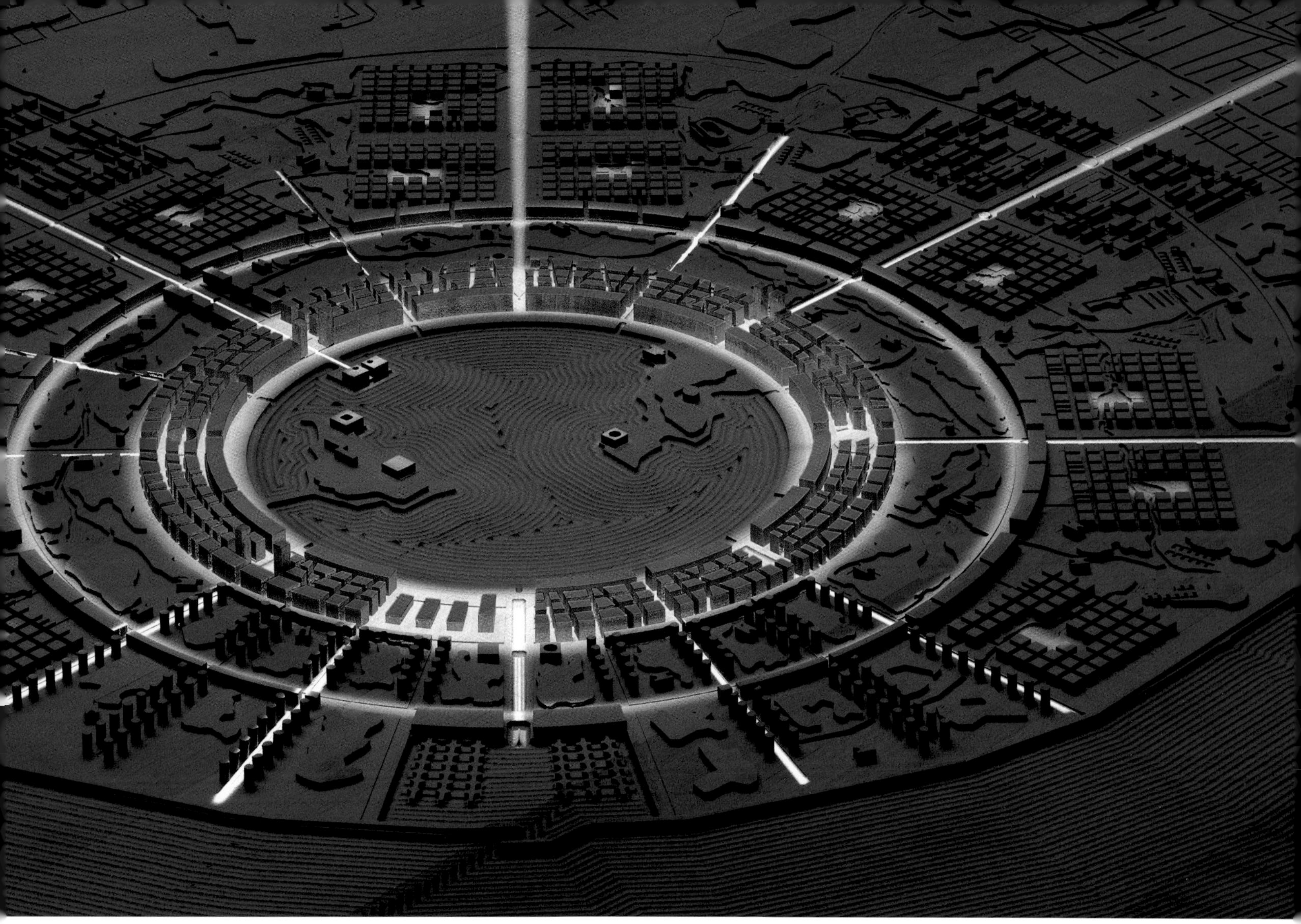

"The concept of Luchao Harbour City takes up the ideal of the traditional European city and combines it with a 'revolutionary idea': instead of a high-density center, the focal point will be a circular lake with a diameter of two and a half kilometers and an eight kilometer lakeside promenade with a bathing beach à la Copa Cabana in the heart of the city. Cultural buildings and leisure facilities are located on islands, which can be accessed by boat. The design was inspired by the city of Alexandria, one of the Seven Wonders of the World." (Meinhard von Gerkan)

Wolf Hilbertz

Arche Saya, Saya de Malha Bank, Indian Ocean, 9°11.953′ S, 60°21.002′ E, Since 1997

Like a gleaming white citadel, Arche Saya—an archaic shell structure—rises up from the water. Inside it there is a harbor and a gigantic tidal power station. Along the tops of the walls there are windmills and solar panels. The population of 50,000 inhabitants is entirely self-reliant; their daily diet consists of cultivated sea fruits and fish. Most impressive of all, this island is constructed using building materials that are extracted in situ from the sea using a biochemical calcification process. A by-product of this "biorock" production process is hydrogen, which is successfully exported by the inhabitants of "Autopia."

Arche Saya is not just a vision. After decades of research, in 1997 the German architect and environmental designer Wolf Hilbertz chose a sandbank, Saya de Malha Bank, as the site for the first basic module—a three-meter-high steel pyramid—of his biorock city.

In the early 1970s, as scientists were exploring the oceans as a source of energy and nutrition Wolf Hilbertz discovered that the seas also contain vast amounts of potential building materials: If metal grilles are immersed in salt water and receive an electric charge, chalk deposits will collect on the metal. Depending on the level of the charge and the rate of growth, this method produces either soft brucite or hard aragonite that when mixed together create the perfect building material for a structure that must be both flexible and able to bear extreme loads. The model for the project was the behavior of corals and crustaceans, which naturally exploit the electrical and biological potential of salt water to create coral atolls, the largest organic architectural structures on Earth.

Arche Saya is a project designed for both humans and marine fauna, but particularly for reef-building polyps. With the rise of ocean temperatures in recent decades, 27 percent of coral reefs have been destroyed. Research into the possible regeneration of corals has shown that coral-producing polyps can find a new habitat in the electrified metal grilles and grow four times faster there than in their natural surroundings.

This biorock city deserves the name ecopolis since it contributes to maintaining the natural balance in the environment. While the production of cement generates about 10 percent of the world's greenhouse gases, this new building material is CO_2 neutral. Solar panels can easily supply the low level of electricity needed for the steel constructions.

Arche Saya marks the beginning of an ecological revolution at sea which, in Wolf Hilbertz' words, is "gently sustained by global biochemical cycles, without destroying the natural balance of the elements."

Arche Saya is a concept for a city that starts its life under water as an artificial coral reef. Steel mats, positioned in the sea and supplied with an electric current, gradually become coated in chalk deposits. The "biorock" produced by this method is used to build the city above water. In addition the biorock structures support coral gardens which are vital to endangered coral fauna.

Jean Hugues Tricard and DL2A Didier Lefort Architectes Associés

Hotel Le Meridien, Bora Bora, French Polynesia, 1998

The more technology dominates our everyday lives, the more a countercurrent of "back to nature" can be felt. The waters of Polynesia undoubtedly rank as some of the loveliest on earth. Towards the end of the nineteenth century, the painterly eye of Paul Gauguin put Tahiti on the map of world-weary Europeans. In one of his South Sea paintings, of 1892, the artist asks *Parau Api* (What's New?). The answer is—a lot! On the southern tip of the ten-kilometer-long coral island of Motu Piti Aau, which can be reached in twenty minutes from the airport of Bora Bora or from Tahiti, a dream has come true: a luxury hotel on stilts in the turquoise blue lagoon with its white sandy beaches.

Each of the eighty-five wooden bungalows consists of a spacious bedroom/sitting room, a bath with a view of the lagoon, and a terrace with a jetty and steps leading down into the water. After taking a dip in the Pacific as though it were a private swimming pool, guests can lounge under the reed awning in front of the bungalow or admire the bright underwater world through the glass floor inside. The exotic appeal of these holiday homes on stilts lies in the combination of elegant European design with authentic Polynesian art, rooted in Africa and South America.

The rates for accommodation are not exactly cheap, but the experience is certainly worth it. In this South Sea paradise, a complex has been built in wonderful harmony with the forces of nature. The French architecture and interior design firm DL2A Didier Lefort designed the hotel down to the last detail. Jean Hugues Tricard was the architect on site.

This hotel offers the perfect blend of nature and luxury. Each guest has a private chalet in the lagoon, set far enough apart to provide a real sense of privacy.

The Palm Jumeirah, 2001–2006, The Palm Jebel Ali, 2002–2007 The Palm Deira, since 2004, The World, 2003–2005

Dubai, United Arab Emirates

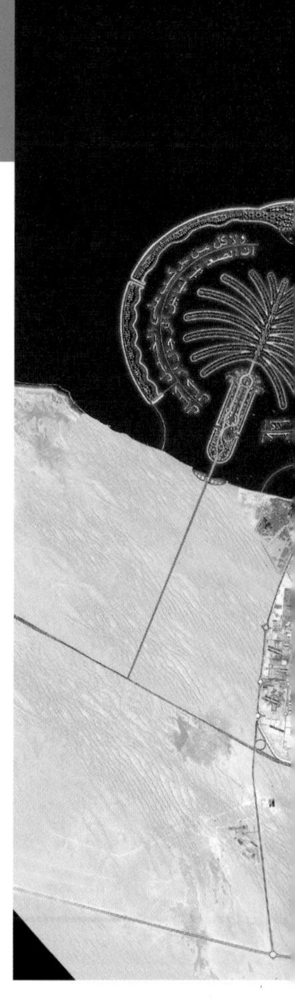

The palm frond is a symbol of eternal life and a promise of a land of plenty. The man-made island off the coast of Jumeirah in the shape of a palm tree, reclaimed by enormous dredgers, promises no less. An earthly paradisiacal retreat, it offers an abundance of natural beauty, seclusion, and luxury. The Palm Jumeirah residences were all sold within a matter of weeks.

Sheltered by a breakwater crescent the crown of the palm spreads its seventeen sweeping fronds, which collectively house more than 2,000 residences with private beaches and tropical gardens. Some sixty luxury theme hotels are being built on the breakwater island, with facilities and fittings designed to reflect the cultures of different countries. Those seeking contact with the outside world will find all the services they require by taking a trip to the trunk of the palm, a long and narrow island with an urban infrastructure of hotels, shopping malls, banks, and medical facilities.

A second palm island, Jebel Ali, is already under construction fifteen kilometers west of Jumeirah. The Palm Jebel Ali—40 percent larger than Jumeirah—is encircled by an additional man-made island with curved jetties that spell out a poem in Arabic legible from the air. A third and even bigger project is already being planned: Palm Deira, with more than 7,000 villas on 41 palm fronds.

GPS technology was used for the complex calculations involved in creating these palm-shaped forms in the sea. Construction of the fifteen-meter-deep foundations proved even more difficult. Dutch expertise in land reclamation was called upon, tides and currents monitored, and a tailor-made system of layered stone was developed to withstand even the heaviest flooding. Calculations have also taken into account the effects of climate change on sea levels.

Yet another project is underway based on the same principle: The World, a man-made archipelago of three hundred islands in the form of a world map situated four kilometers off the coast of Dubai.

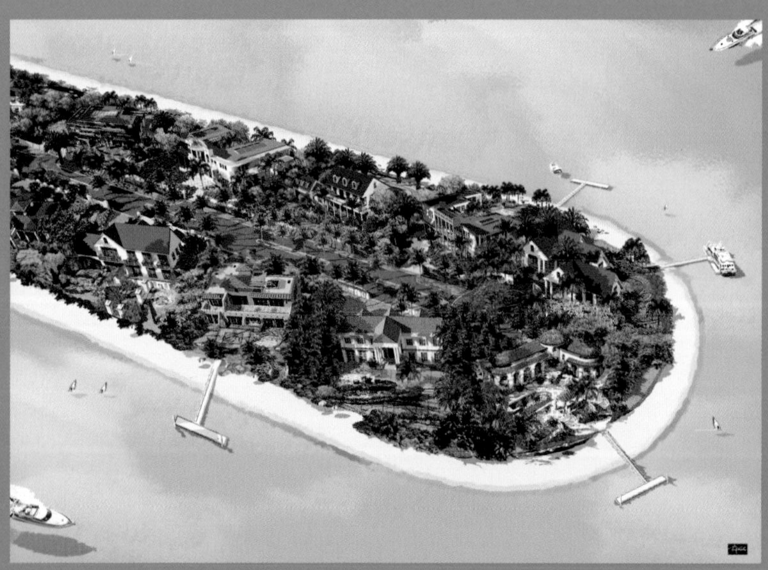

The sharp contours of the man-made islands Jumeirah (left) and Jebel Ali (right) in the Arabian Gulf are visible with the naked eye from outer space and have already been hailed by the media as the Eighth Wonder of the World. A third palm-shaped project, Palm Deira, is already planned.

The palm shape is not only decorative, but also adds hundreds of extra kilometres of sandy beaches to the seventy-two kilometres of existing beach of this tiny emirate. Almost near completion by the same developer, Sheikh Mohammed, is an archipelago of 300 islands in the shape of a map of the world.

For centuries, people have lived in homes floating on water. The best known of these is the classic houseboat, which is probably the first image to come to mind. But we have gone a step further and have included a colorful range of floating constructions where people could live—at least temporarily. As the number of people who want to live on water is steadily increasing, architects are meeting their demands with a variety of concepts ranging from small settlements to floating towns with thousands of inhabitants. Floating homes can also be created by converting commercial vessels into loftboats, with the hull now acting as no more than a pontoon, a shell. By their nature, these homes are lofts with the atmosphere of a ship. All these ideas testify to the advent of a new lifestyle where people live permanently on water and realize their dream of a floating nest.

Floating Homes

1234

Lehigh Valley Railroad Barge #79

Red Hook, Brooklyn, New York, USA, 1914

In the mid-nineteenth century, the swamps of the booming industrial region of Brooklyn on the waterfront of the East River and New York Harbor were drained to build what was at the time a highly modern port complex. Today, empty brick warehouses bear witness to its golden age.

Thanks to a number of cultural and entrepreneurial initiatives, the urban waterfront is gradually shaking off its image of crisis and deprivation. One of the major attractions is the Lehigh Valley Railroad Barge #79 moored at Red Hook since 1998, restored and maintained by the Sharp family as a historic monument. It is not actually possible to live on the barge; official permission is not available in New York City where, unlike earthquake-prone San Francisco, there is no tradition of houseboats.

Barges were used until the 1950s by the railroad companies to transport goods on the Hudson River. Artist David Sharps discovered the abandoned barge in 1984 mired in the mudflats near the George Washington Bridge. Sharps set about freeing the barge from three hundred tons of mud and restoring it. His search for a mooring place was fraught with difficulty and the high costs of anchorage fees forced him to move the barge repeatedly until he finally found a permanent home for it at the historic piers of Red Hook, Brooklyn.

The two-story barge, ten meters wide and thirty meters long, has little in common with the comfortably equipped vessels that ply the rivers of Europe. The substructure, crudely built of heavy beams, seems to have more in common with log cabins than shipbuilding. The superstructure, which does not even keep the wind out, is lacking all architectural pretense. The toilets still operate with the pre-industrial technology of buckets and tanks. This however contributes to the authentic historical atmosphere of the barge which boasts one unparalleled advantage over any building on land: wide, uninterrupted views of the Statue of Liberty and the Manhattan skyline.

The Lehigh Valley Railroad Barge #79, built in 1914, transported cargo on the Hudson River until the 1950s. Built of heavy wooden beams, it is a purely functional structure that offers its users nothing in the way of creature comforts. Now recognized as a historic monument, the barge is currently moored at Red Hook, Brooklyn, where it is a popular attraction of the community for cultural activities.

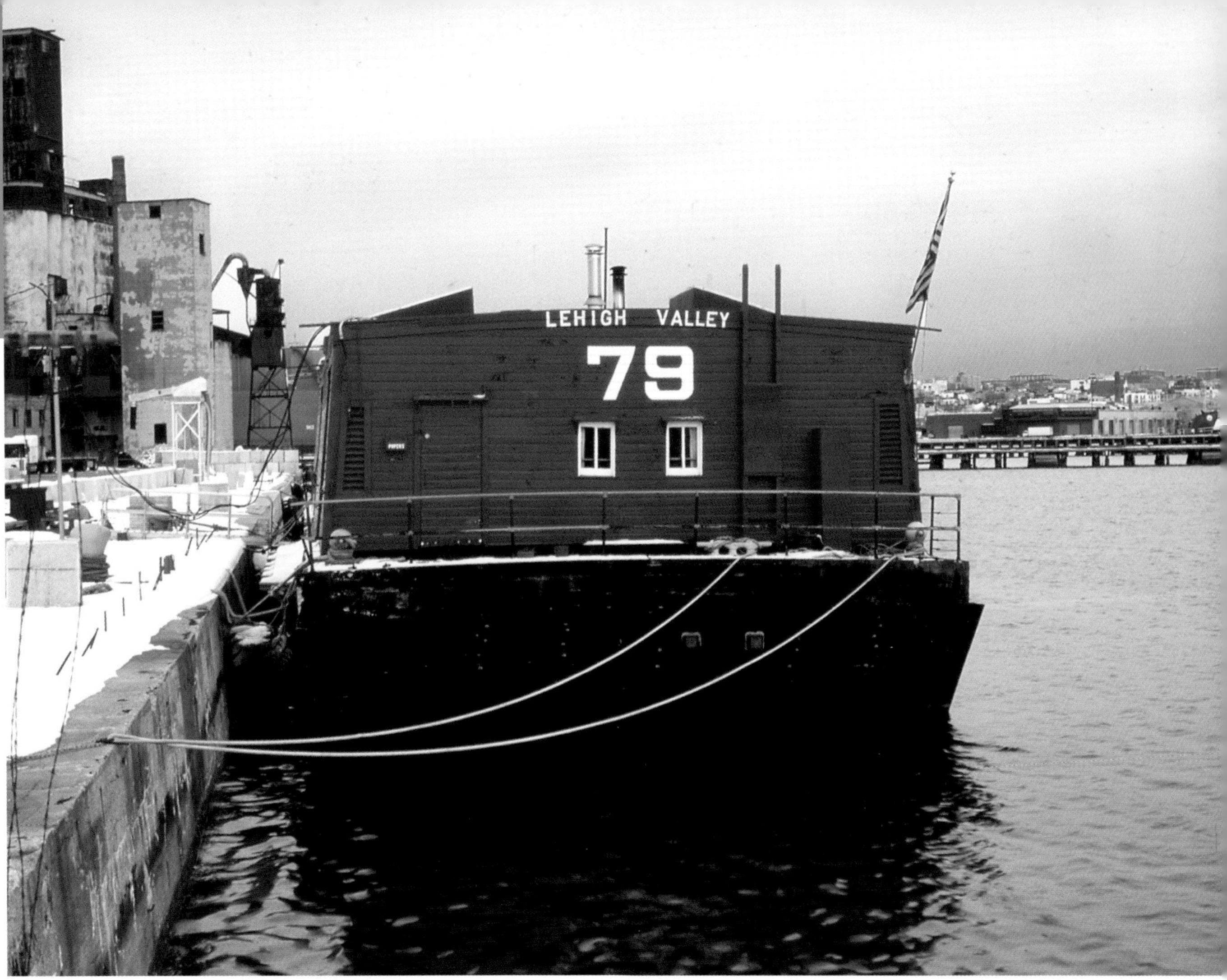
LEHIGH VALLEY
79

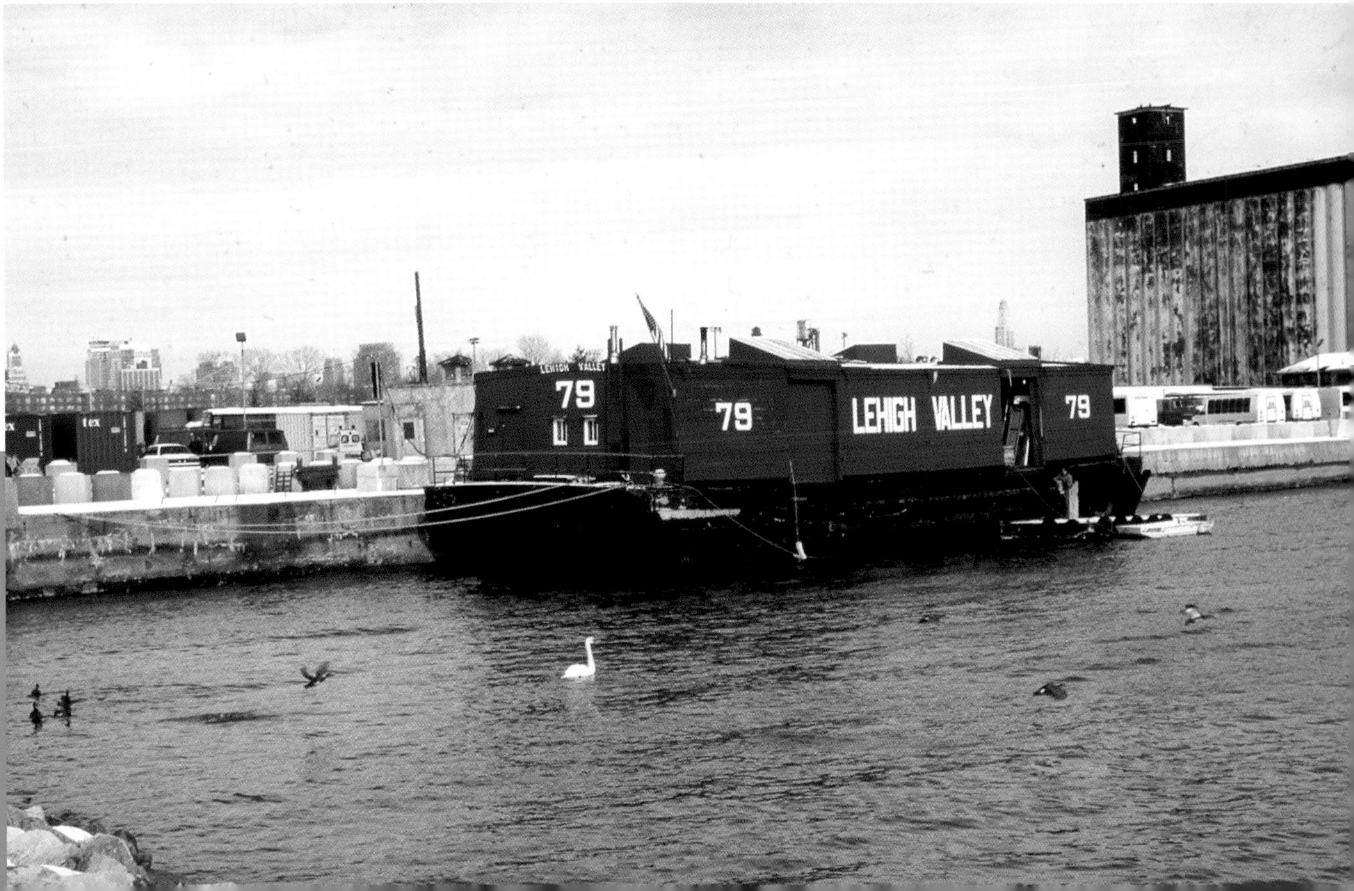
LEHIGH VALLEY
79
79
LEHIGH VALLEY
79

Walter Bettens and Siegrid Demyttenaere

Ship-ping, Ghent, Belgium, Construction 1957, Conversion 1999–2000

There is something heavy and cumbersome about the look of a barge. Its long, low body and broad bow is the very opposite of the sharply streamlined styling of a yacht. Barges smell of diesel and tar, and bear the traces of their countless journeys along rivers and canals to the industrial centers of Europe—a nomadic life that is a law unto itself, seemingly untouched by the hustle and bustle of the city. Yet it is these very factors that give the barges their strange appeal. At the end of their working life decommissioned barges quite often find buyers willing to restore them painstakingly as riverboat homes with incomparable interiors.

One fascinating example is the conversion of the Ship-ping barge by Belgian designers Walter Bettens and Siegrid Demyttenaere. They have transformed the thirty-nine-meter-long by five-meter-wide body of the barge into a long, open-plan space for working and living. The portholes with their heavy brass fittings and the visible ribs of the walls remind us that we are on the water. The planked flooring recalls a ship's deck. The water tank is concealed behind a library of dark-stained wood, above which there is a cleverly designed mezzanine floor with conference table.

The Ship-ping barge conversion shows how the limitations imposed by historic shipbuilding design challenge architects to come up with particularly original solutions.

After fifty years spent plying the waterways of Europe, the old Ship-ping barge is now moored at Ghent. Belgian architects Walter Bettens and Siegrid Demyttenaere have lovingly transformed it into a loftboat with a modern interior.

Cuypers & Q Architecten

Eco-tech Loftboat, Ghent, Belgium, Construction 1965, Conversion 2000–2004

From today's vantage point, there is something idyllic about old barges. We tend to associate them with the romantic freedom of plying the rivers and canals, forgetting the hard life of the crews that manned these vessels that were designed for the purely economic premise of the transportation of goods, and offering little in the way of creature comforts.

Is it possible to merge the idyllic image with modern standards of living? The Antwerp-based group of architects Gert Cuypers, Raf De Preter, and Ilze Quaeyhaegens has done so with aplomb. Their conversion of a disused barge into a loftboat contrasts the clear lines of modern interior design in spacious rooms with the archaic forms of the boat. One of the most striking features is the slanted glass structure on deck that houses the entrance and stairway, serving as a skylight for the central studio and living room below deck while screening the interior from the shore. A long wall of built-in storage links the living room with the kitchen. Glass partitions with venetian blinds separate the bedroom from the bathroom and work spaces.

The cutting edge eco-technology includes a garden on the upper deck, with lava stones and succulents, as a wastewater treatment plant.

At night, the loftboat forms a romantic backdrop by the jetty. When the people living on the barge look out of the window, what they see is not traffic rushing past, but the broken pools of light from their window reflecting on the water.

The Eco-tech Loftboat combines the romanticism of the barge with modern loft architecture and an ecological ethos. The garden on deck serves as a wastewater treatment plant.

N55

Spaceframe and Floating Platform, Copenhagen, Denmark, 1999

N55 is a group of young architects and artists from Copenhagen who take their name from their street address (Norre Farigmagsgade 55). Their highly original designs—including an urban garden for paved areas, a factory, and a swap shop—are not for sale, but rather offered free of charge online as DIY instruction manuals. All the group asks for in return is that the finished products are made available to the public.

The versatile modular structure of Spaceframe that can be extended to form a floating home is typical of their approach. This complex structure is made up of flat, stainless steel struts bolted together to form a truncated tetrahedron. The fifty-centimeter-deep wall structure can be filled with insulating material or used for interior fittings such as built-in wardrobes or shelving. The outer skin is constructed of stainless steel panels and the inside of plaster-fiberboard. The floating platform can be assembled using the same system components. Polyethylene plastic tanks, some of them filled with water, are installed between the struts to aid flotation. The use of standard components helps to keep costs low.

Spaceframe was designed for easy assembly and dismantling by practically anyone. Its low-maintenance weatherproof materials and compact components make it economical to run and easy to store; the group's web-site proudly demonstrates all the struts stacked neatly beneath a sofa.

If the unusual Spaceframe design appeals to you, you might be surprised to discover that this floating house is not for sale. This is the group's way of protesting against all forms of commercialization. Apart from images of the prototype, all that is available is a detailed set of online instructions for building it yourself.

Marlies Rohmer

City Hostel, Amsterdam, The Netherlands, Project, 2001–2003

Their feathers dyed in lurid colors, young chicks huddle in a cage, pecking hopelessly at the iron bars. This depressing photo from the design brochure of a new youth hostel in Amsterdam is clearly intended as a critique of conventional youth hostels, but at the same time a reminder of the fact that youth hostels still have to provide cheap accommodation for the masses—particularly for a young, international clientele. In recent decades, the expectations, demands, and lifestyles of this target group have changed considerably.

Dutch architect Marlies Rohmer has come up with the concept of the City Hostel that meets the needs of the twenty-first century youth-hosteller. First of all, location is important. Youth hostels should not be on the outskirts but in the city center, within easy reach of the urban buzz. So Rohmer has taken to the water and has designed a floating complex set in an inland shipping harbor basin in the center of Amsterdam. Because it is on the water, the City Hostel can be designed as a freestanding structure that does not have to take historic buildings and streets into account. The reception, with its spacious lobbies and seating areas, is located on the transparent first level. The sleeping areas on the upper levels are designed to accommodate the different lifestyles of the target clientele. Spread among several levels there are rooms with two to six beds, a hammock area for interrailing backpackers, and space on the roof for groups and individual travelers who prefer to pitch their tents outdoors.

City Hostel guests have access to a hotel website providing information on current room availability as well as the nationalities and interests of the other guests. They can use a secure code to contact each other and arrange meetings or excursions. Close-ups of arriving guests and pictures of their home countries are projected on huge monitors mounted on the facades, conveying hostel life and its international context to the world outside.

In this new youth hostel, interactive information and multimedia take over the traditional role of the hostel director as advisor and coordinator. Whether this is a step towards a more sociable world—or a more anonymous one—remains to be seen.

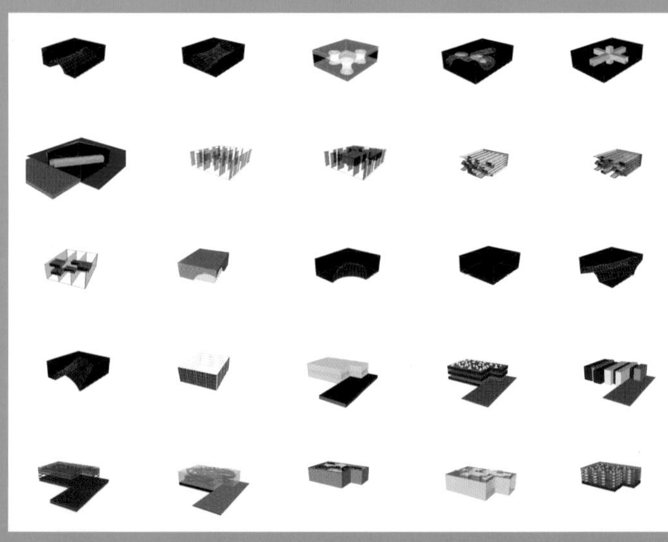

The City Hostel is Amsterdam-based architect Marlies Rohmer's vision for a new youth hostel in Houthaven, Amsterdam, with a boat jetty and direct access to the city center. This floating complex with its multimedia facade caters to tourists with different lifestyles. One level houses traditional dormitories, another hammocks, and the rooftop a campsite.

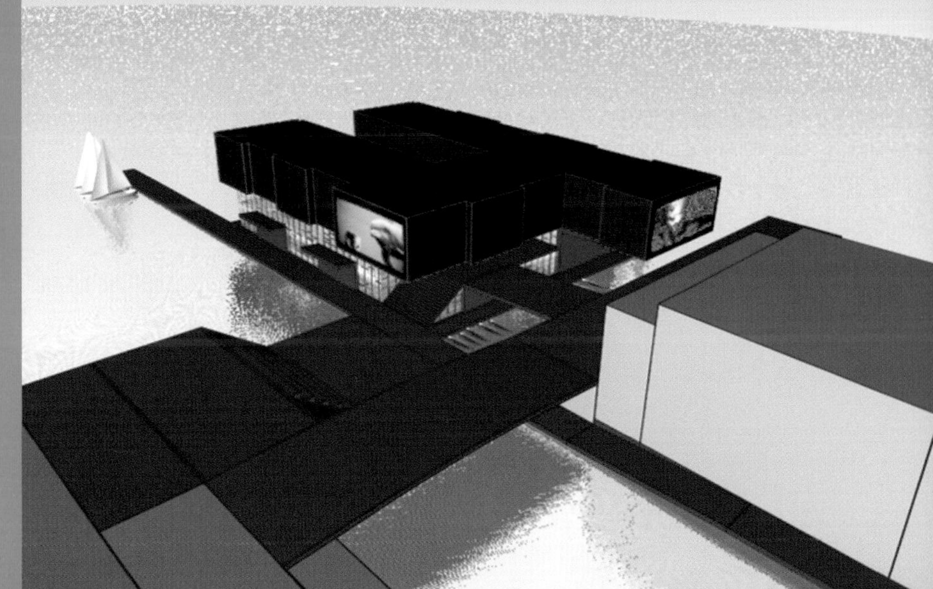

Architectuurstudio Herman Hertzberger

Watervilla Middelburg, De Veersche Poort, Middelburg, The Netherlands, 2002
Semi-Waterhouses, Ypenburg, The Netherlands, Since 1998

Holland has a long tradition of houseboats, born of necessity. Water, after all, covers almost 18 percent of this densely populated country. Small wonder, then, that the renowned Dutch architect Herman Hertzberger has also designed water houses. His latest design, the Watervilla Middelburg, was built as a prototype in 2002. The water house stands on a hexagonal pontoon of ballast-filled steel tubes that also provide walk-in storage space. Based on the same principle as offshore drilling platforms, the weighted substructure design supports up to 135 tons and stabilizes the superstructure in high winds and rough water.

The three stories of this dwelling are playfully stacked one on top of another. Each story has its own spacious patio, creating a fluid transition between the interior and the exterior. In the prototype, the bedrooms and bathroom are located on the ground floor, which is linked by a spiral staircase to the living and dining area on the middle floor. The top floor can be used as a studio or office space. All possible options have not yet been realized in this building. The house has a variable floorplan, and depending on the occupants, optional features can be added later.

Stylistically, this is a house in the spirit of classical modernism. Reduced to recognizable geometric elements, its overall appearance is enlivened by angular and rounded components. One particularly striking feature of the Watervilla is the fact that it can rotate 110 degrees to make the most of the sunshine during the changing seasons. The technical facilities require that the house be connected to an infrastructure near the shore.

The entire project can be assembled over a period of four months using prefabricated parts. Though construction costs are somewhat higher than for a conventional house, this was compensated by saving on the price of a mainland building site.

In contrast to the floating Watervilla, Hertzberger designed the Semi-Waterhouses project as a densely populated settlement. This complex for inland waters does not float on the water, but on a concrete island. The island stands on the ground below water and can be used as an underground garage. The diagonally-set living rooms offer fantastic views over the water.

When land is at a premium, why not live on the water? Amsterdam architect Herman Hertzberger has developed different concepts for inland waters. His Semi-Waterhouses form a compact settlement of several houses built on a firm sunken foundation that serves as an underground garage. The Watervilla stands on a hexagonal pontoon and is a floating house island.

Grüntuch Ernst Architects

Floating Homes, Berlin, Germany, Project, 2002

Berlin is crisscrossed by a network of lakes, rivers, and canals so extensive that you could take an all-day cruise without ever setting foot on dry land. In the past, craftsmen and factories settled on the shores of these waterways, but as industry moved out to the periphery and became increasingly reliant on road transport, new development opportunities emerged along the waterfronts. Today, the city authorities envision creating leisure facilities and small-scale residential districts with water houses.

The planned groups of eight to twelve units offer exclusive accommodation without encroaching on the promenades. The complexes are separated by broad expanses of water. Houseboats are integrated into a harbor setting with jetties forming the urban structure. One of the winners of the competition for the Rummelsburger Bucht development is the Berlin-based firm of Armand Grüntuch and Almut Ernst. The non-motorized houseboat is just 7.5 meters wide and 4.4 meters high so that it can pass through all the city's canals and locks. There are three zones: the middle deck with its spacious living and dining area is accessed directly from the jetty and a glass partition opens onto a terrace overlooking the lake. Below deck are the sleeping areas and sanitary facilities in a cabin-style layout with portholes; and the upper deck, accessed by an external stairway, forms a sundeck for dining under the stars with panoramic views, fitted with glass windbreakers for comfort and privacy.

Those who still yearn for a garden of their own can dock onto an island pontoon that doubles as a child's playground and jetty.

Berlin is a city with hundreds of kilometers of shorelines where the local authorities are now helping to fund the development of small-scale water house settlements. The aim is to provide affordable waterfront living without building on the actual shore, retaining the promenades as public leisure areas. This concept can of course be applied to any waterside city, such as Venice.

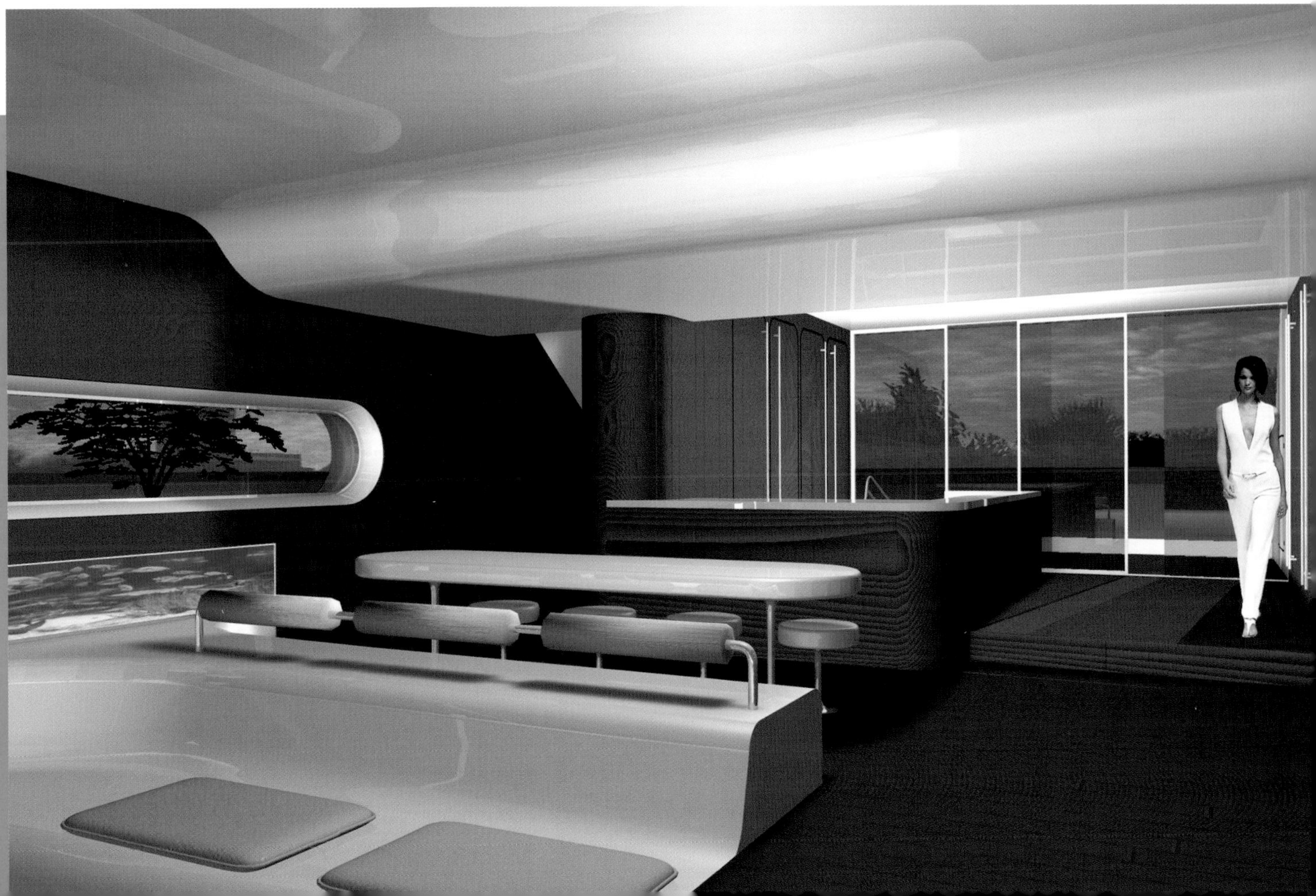

Förster Trabitzsch Architects

Floating Homes H2O, Berlin, Germany, 2002–2005

For all its many seas and rivers, Germany has no tradition of living on the water. Enjoying the tranquility of a houseboat is seen mainly as a leisure activity, as something to do on holiday in the Netherlands or France. Now, the cities of Hamburg and Berlin are aiming to change all that by introducing large-scale urban developments on the water in a way that enriches the quality of life without adversely affecting the shorelines and waterfronts.

In the year 2005, one of the first of these water developments is to be built on a lovely lake formed by the River Havel in Berlin's Spandau district. Among the winners of the Europe-wide design competition are Hamburg-based architects Martin Förster and Karsten Trabitzsch with their futuristic-looking Floating Home H2O. The spacious structure on three levels is set on a reinforced concrete pontoon system that does not envision any underwater facilities. The curves and angles of the dual steel shells that house the light-flooded living and sleeping areas give the Floating Home its elegant appearance. Because the lightweight walls have no load-bearing function, the system permits a flexible layout.

The water developments—up to twelve units linked by jetties—form small harbors. As an apartment on the water is considerably more expensive than a conventional one on dry land, anyone planning to purchase a property in a water village must be genuinely enthusiastic about living so close to the elements.

Transparency is the key feature of the Floating Home H2O by Förster Trabitzsch Architects. The fluid transition between interior and exterior gives the residents the feeling of living outdoors.

Waterstudio

Wo29 Lounger, Ijburg, The Netherlands, Project, 2002–2005

The architects and designers of the Dutch firm Waterstudio offer floating houses such as the Wo29 Lounger, as well as floating exhibition venues, business streets, and even churches. A little village on the water can be created in modular, building-block style—and it surely won't be long before floating cinemas and athletic fields are added.

The Wo29 Lounger project with its angular superstructures recalls a motorboat, but is actually a spacious houseboat. The rooftop terrace kitchen with its broad glass dome is like the command center of a spaceship. Here, the cook feels like the captain—but stirring rather than steering. In fine weather, cooking and eating are al fresco. The spacious living and sleeping area is on the ground level below. Like houses on land, water houses also need a substantial foundation and in the case of the Lounger, a cast concrete pontoon ensures the necessary stability and compensation for wave movement.

The idea behind the Lounger project is the dream of young Dutch architects and designers Koen Olthuis, J. D. Peereboom Voller, and Marjolein Kreuk to create an affordable mass-produced water house. In principle, this is not new. Many homes on land and water are assembled using prefabricated components. What is new about the Lounger is that the metal outer skin can be produced in large quantities, like the chassis of a car. The interior, including the layout and choice of materials, is left entirely to the taste and preferences of the client.

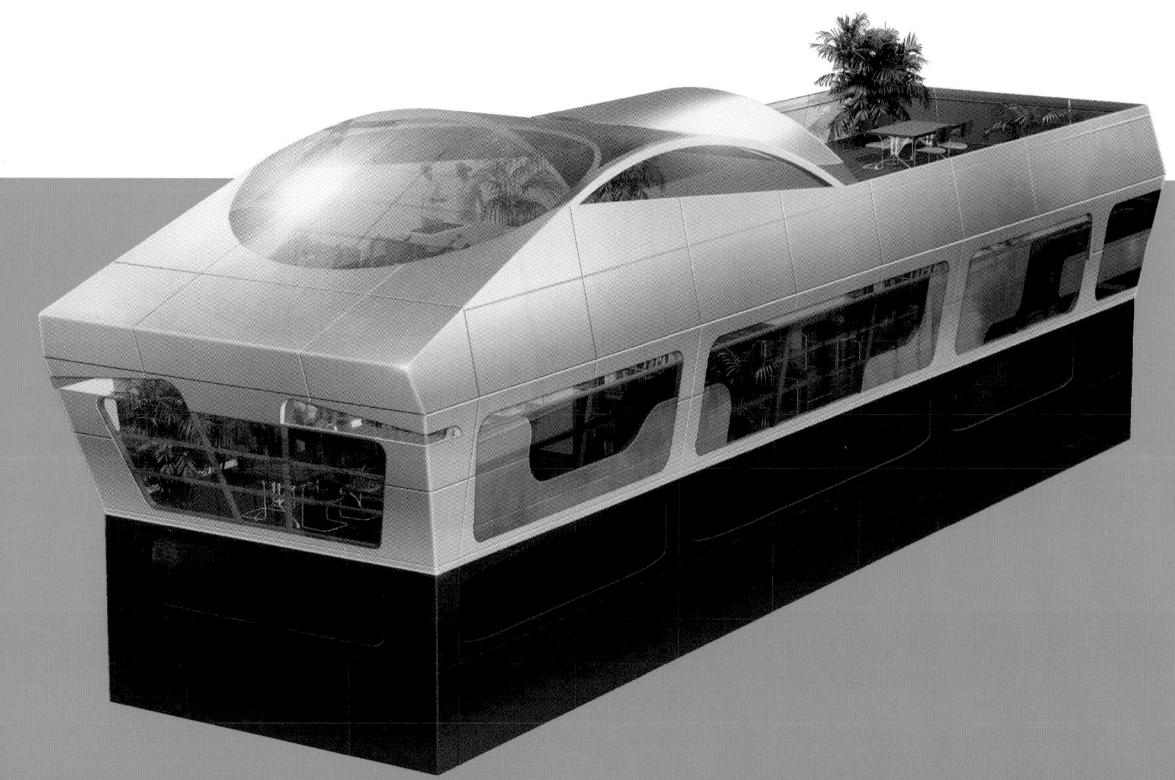

The Wo29 Lounger is a spacious houseboat offering all the creature comforts desired in northern Europe. The kitchen has a special place on the uppermost level under a glass dome that naturally keeps cooking odors out of the living area.

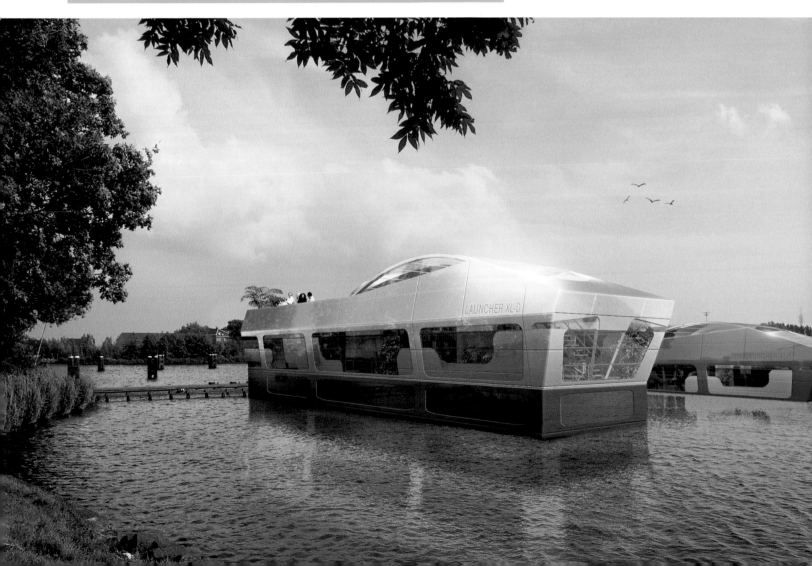

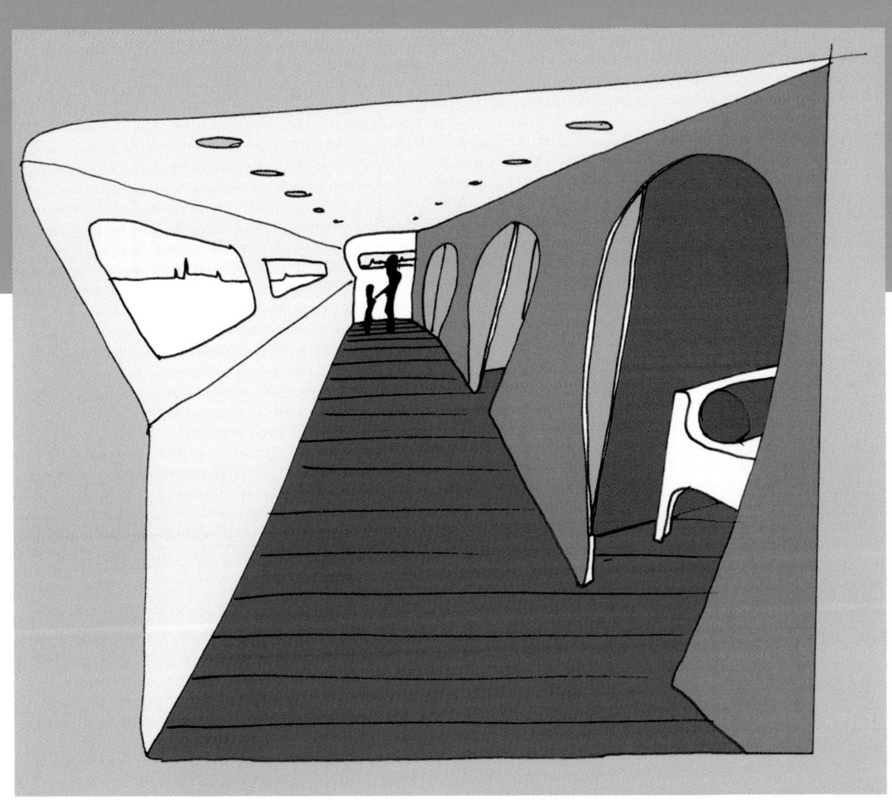

Jord den Hollander

Woonark, Amsterdam, The Netherlands, 2000–2002

This extraordinary house does seem to hover about a meter above the water—as though it was lying on a cushion of air by day and a cushion of light by night. This effect is created by a narrow ribbon of windows on the waterline through which there is an uninterrupted view.

This perplexing play between illusion and reality was designed by the famous Amsterdam architect and filmmaker Jord den Hollander. His works are not only spatial concepts, but are also based on a cinemato-graphic handling of light.

In spite of this unusual approach, Woonark is an example of highly functional waterhouse architecture. By raising the box-like structure ninety centimeters above the water, the bedrooms and bathrooms of the floating concrete hull are provided with a ribbon window affording fantastic frog's-eye views of the water world. The spacious living room on the upper deck has large sliding doors almost the entire length of the wall. When they are opened in summer, the living room extends to a floating veranda.

The use of light by the film director and architect is evident both inside and out. The walls are clad in weatherproof polycarbonate. Daylight flowing through the opaque outer skin hits a green membrane that makes the waterhouse shimmer in gentle greenish hues. The back wall of the kitchen is an opaque glass wall with a narrow window aperture looking out onto the canal. With its glass objects on the windowsill, it forms a modern Dutch still life.

Amsterdam architect and filmmaker Jord den Hollander describes the concept behind his Woonark waterhouse as a play of light and gravity. The polycarbonate-clad structure seems to hover on its glass base.

Marlies Rohmer

Water Dwellings, Amsterdam, The Netherlands, Project, 2001–2003

The Ijsselmeer, sheltered from the stormy North Sea by a protective dyke built in 1932, lies to the northeast of Amsterdam. In the course of time, the sea has been pushed back by the rivers that flow into it, so that today the Ijsselmeer is Europe's biggest freshwater reservoir, providing more than 50 percent of the country's water supply. It also offers the potential of new residential development in Europe's most densely populated country. Amsterdam-based architect Marlies Rohmer has developed a modular system of floating homes for a number of man-made islands near the city.

This projected urban development on the water is a brightly colored array of seventy-five units that can be constructed either as dyke houses on stilts or as floating homes. They are built on three levels, the first of which is a partly submerged concrete tank lit only by a narrow ribbon of windows. This is where the bedrooms are situated, which need relatively little heating. On top of this is a lightweight steel frame in which wall panels of plastic or glass can be mounted. The cool industrial look is compensated by the design flexibility and freedom of choice in assembling the modular components. The modules can be spaced to create a central atrium housing the stairway or a small wintergarden. Balconies, patios, and awnings can be added—even after completion. Large concrete tanks for as many as three accommodation blocks provide public spaces. The modular system also allows for considerable financial flexibility, from low-income public housing to high-end private homes.

For Marlies Rohmer, this development is not just a project based on the maxim that form follows function and budget, but is the realization of a dream of living on the water: "A boat moored by the house, jetties, sense of individuality, clouds, space, contact with the elements, feeding swans from the kitchen window, ice-skating around the house."

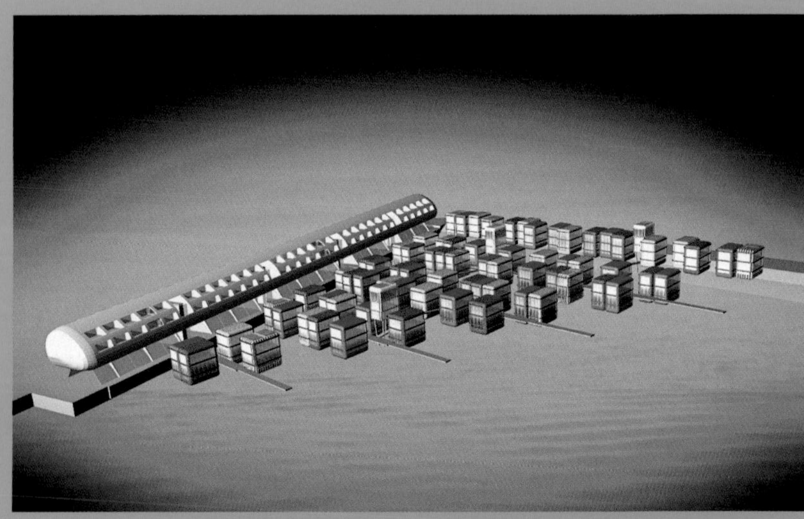

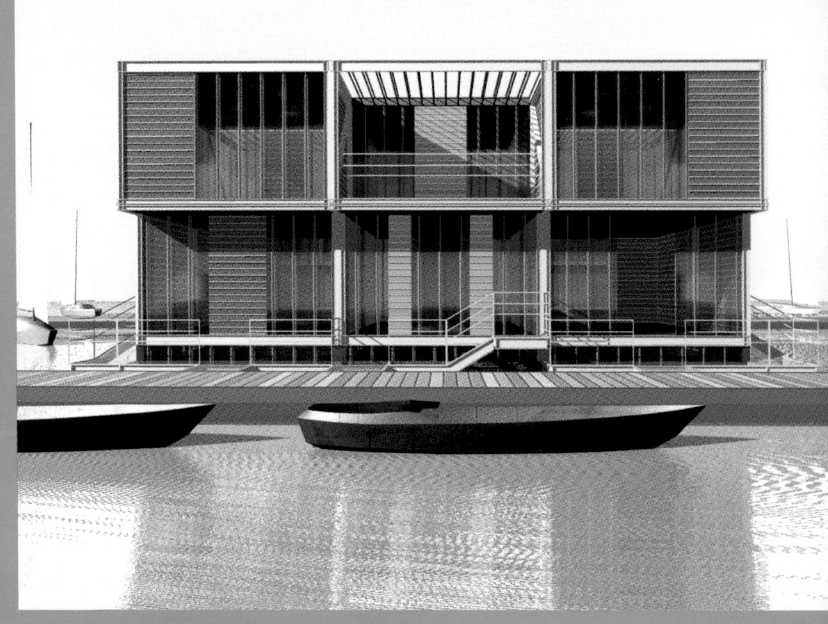

The Water Dwellings project provides for compact development of a piece of water off a man-made island in the IJsselmeer near Amsterdam. Each water house has a jetty and mooring place for exploring the area by boat or simply dropping in on the neighbors for coffee. Suspended power lines crisscross this waterbound urban development diagonally, creating a triangular layout.

Floating Houses

British Columbia, Canada

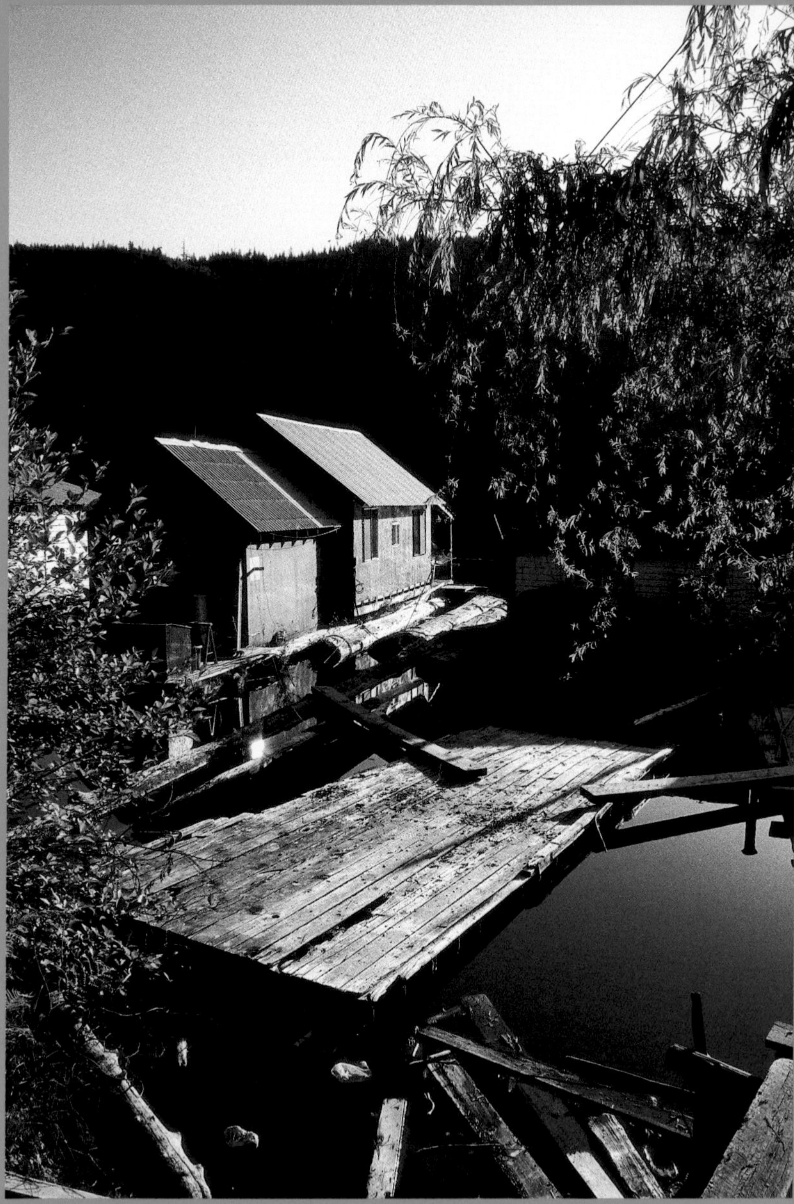

In northwestern British Columbia, where the vast forests have made timber a major industry, there have always been floating houses. Log cabins—built on rafts as camps for the families of the lumberjacks—have their own plant and machinery and even a service station. There are communal cooking and laundry facilities, workshops, and storage depots for gasoline and other necessities. In former times, these camps consisted of ten to twenty rafts built of thick cedar trunks, with a life expectancy of some twenty-five years, and were moved from one area to the next as the forests were cleared. But with the march of progress—lightweight boats, powerful outboard motors, and seaplanes—people are more willing to travel longer distances to work. As the mobility of these camps is no longer as important as it once was, they grow bigger and more fully equipped.

City dwellers in search of rural tranquility have long since discovered the floating weekend home as an alternative to a more land-bound holiday cottage, but now they need not go without such creature comforts as electricity. Instead of simple log cabins, wood-clad houses in typical American style are now being built, with every conceivable interior fitting. With no planning constraints and no architects' fees, nature-loving DIY enthusiasts can hammer together a roof over their heads using natural materials. One advantage of this is that a floating home makes only a small and easily reparable intervention in the environment and can be completely dismantled for disposal—if one does not want to wait for nature to do the demolition job itself.

These incredibly flexible homes can be built in any way and turned to face any direction in order to make the most of the view or the sunshine. Moving house does not even involve packing boxes—just take the whole house with you. And if you need more space, you can add on a second raft.

Jean-Michel Ducancelle

Anthenea Aquasphere, No Fixed Location, Launched 2001

In *The Spy Who Loved Me*, James Bond and his sidekick use a luxuriously high-tech life capsule to escape a watery grave. This cinematic vision inspired French naval architect Jean-Michel Ducancelle to design a fully fitted, spherical floating island capable of deployment on the high seas. The result is a fantastic saucer-shaped habitat by the name of Anthenea that is brilliantly innovative in its multifunctionality. There is now an "Anthenea Family" with models available in three sizes.

The target group is not the jet set, but rather the growing ecotourism market made up of individuals in search of environmentally sustainable accommodation in tropical waters. The floating islands generate their own energy supply and generate neither noise nor waste. They even have their own wastewater treatment plant.

The basic Anthenea Studio module is a bachelor suite that can also accommodate two. One special feature is the broad, two-part circular pad that acts as a structural stabilizer. It serves as a sun terrace and work platform as well as providing extra storage space. A large glass window in the floor provides views of the underwater world. The interior is like a miniature hotel room complete with kitchen, toilet, shower, and the comforts of climate control and a home entertainment system. At the push of a button the round tabletop in the central dining and sitting area—with its wrap-round panoramic windows—is transformed into a spacious sleeping area.

Rounded forms are a major design feature in the overall layout and in the fine detail, creating a radical aesthetic that stands in contrast to land-based architecture. In terms of technology, the spherical form of the capsule provides optimal thermal insulation—typically a major problem of living on the water.

Aquaspheres can be specially fitted as diving platforms or floating laboratories for coral reefs. The recently developed larger-scale models—with a diameter of more than ten meters—provide all the comforts of a family home on two levels. Ducancelle envisions small settlements of Anthenea units like water lilies on a pond. If necessary, they can be placed on land using inflatable cushions and launched elsewhere the following day.

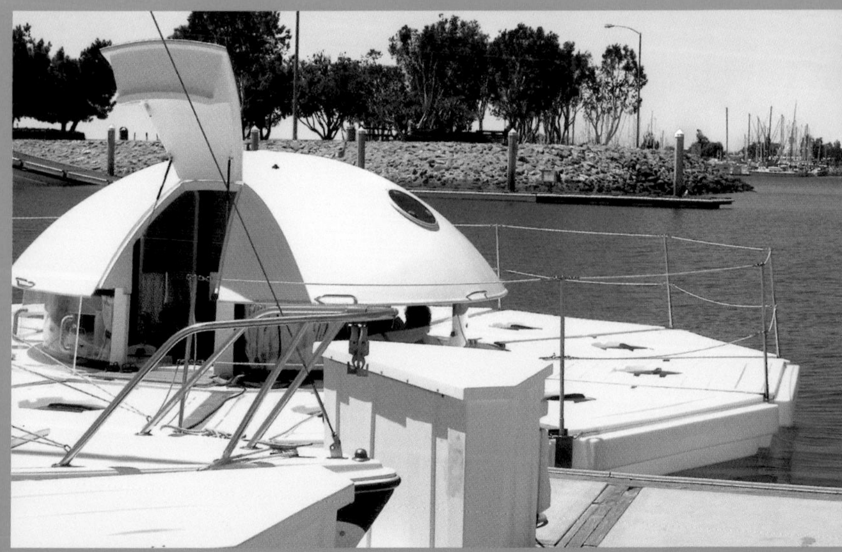

You do not need a sailing certificate or even a zoning permit for an Aquasphere. These futuristic islands are self-contained accommodation units with their own solar energy, rainwater purification, and sewage treatment. French naval architect Jean-Michel Ducancelle spent seven years developing these floating holiday homes.

Jean-Michel Ducancelle
Anthenea Aquasphere, No Fixed Location, Launched 2001

Aquaspheres allow a temporary village to be constructed in a sheltered lagoon. The biggest version is the Aquasphere King, large enough for a water restaurant seating 170 guests.

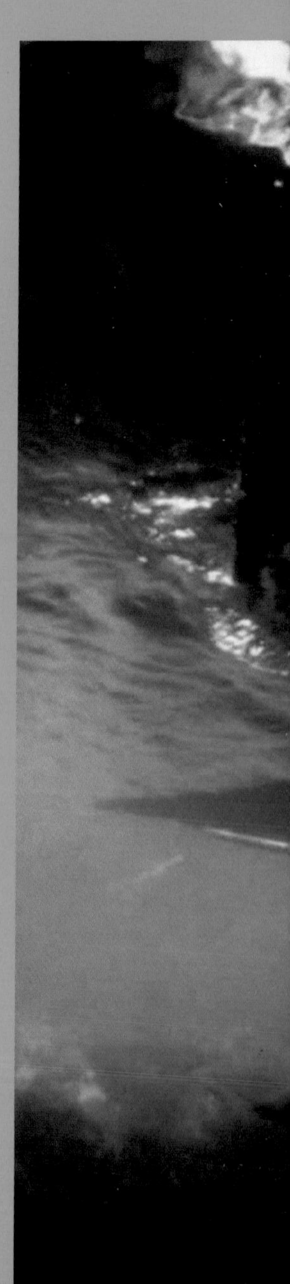

Waki Zöllner

Atoll, Travemünde, Germany, 1965–1978
Floatel 2000, Project, 1989

In the 1970s windsurfing became a popular sport in Europe that gave youngsters a sense of boundless freedom amid the waves and the winds. When Munich designer and artist Waki Zöllner presented his prototypes of a floating island in the form of an oversized life belt in 1978, he struck a chord with the spirit of the times. The dream island of fiberglass-reinforced polyester, by the name of Atoll, was a sensation. It was anchored off the Baltic resort of Travemünde in northern Germany, where it became famous as "the plastic island for eating, bathing, drinking, and dancing." When the island was damaged in the winter of 1979, it went into service off the coast of Kiel, Germany for another ten years as a research station for fish farming in the Baltic. No other models were built.

The ring-shaped island, Atoll, had an external diameter of twenty-seven meters. The main body had sundecks, changing rooms, toilets, a restaurant, and storage spaces. In the center was a circular "lagoon" protected by an underwater net stabilized with fifty tons of ballast. At night, the island became a water disco for two hundred revelers.

Zöllner, who had made a name for himself with his design for the BMW Museum in Munich, was not motivated by the idea of creating recreational islands, but by the vision of living on the water. On the basis of his experience with the Atoll project, Zöllner went on to design Floatel 2000, a floating city for two thousand inhabitants. The island is based on the same design principle as the initial Atoll prototype. A ring-shaped pontoon holds the structures and the infrastructure. The center remains open and can be used for various purposes, like an atrium. The complex is sheltered by a transparent dome that can be opened. The serious shortage of accommodation during the 1992 Barcelona Olympics prompted the idea of building a Floatel complex to be anchored five hundred meters outside the port.

Descriptions of living and working on simple rafts inspired Munich designer Waki Zöllner to design floating islands. The Atoll island in the form of a huge life belt made of polyester and fiberglass became famous as a recreation island and later served a further ten years as a research station in the Baltic Sea.

Zodiac International

Throw-over Life Raft

It had been a wonderful day for diving among the reefs, as the members of the diving excursion recall. In the afternoon, they had phoned their friends in Hamburg to tell them all about it. That night, a storm came up and drove the ship onto the reef, where it sank within minutes. The little group of six managed to clamber onto a life raft and send a mayday on a mobile phone. Every year, many incidents occur similar to this one. Sometimes survivors on their life rafts are found by sheer chance, weeks after the search has been abandoned, hundreds of nautical miles from the wreckage site.

Many vessels are now fitted with life rafts instead of lifeboats because they take up less space and are ready for use simply by throwing them overboard in an emergency. Standard features include a self-erecting protective canopy, a self-activating signal light, and rainwater collection. In stormy seas, the raft can be hermetically sealed to prevent water from entering. There are fresh air vents and lookout apertures.

The Zodiac Open Sea life raft floats and will open as soon as it hits the water. Its large-volume buoyancy chambers and water ballast pockets fill with water as soon as the raft is inflated, stabilizing it in a swell and facilitating boarding, which can be especially difficult from the water. Because hypothermia is often the most serious problem for shipwreck survivors, the Open Sea life raft has an aluminum-lined, composite foam floor that throws back natural body heat in much the same way as a thermal sleeping bag.

Life rafts have become a familiar feature of modern shipping, as important to a shipwreck survivor as a parachute is to a bailed-out pilot. Even if all else fails, the Open Sea life raft will float and open as soon as it hits the water. The technological details are carefully considered and the life raft itself is built to last. Zodiac provides a twelve-year guarantee on its products and life rafts are available in various sizes that carry anywhere from four to 150 people.

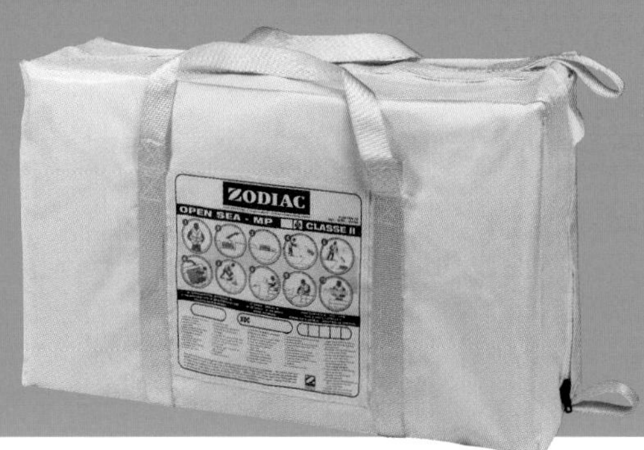

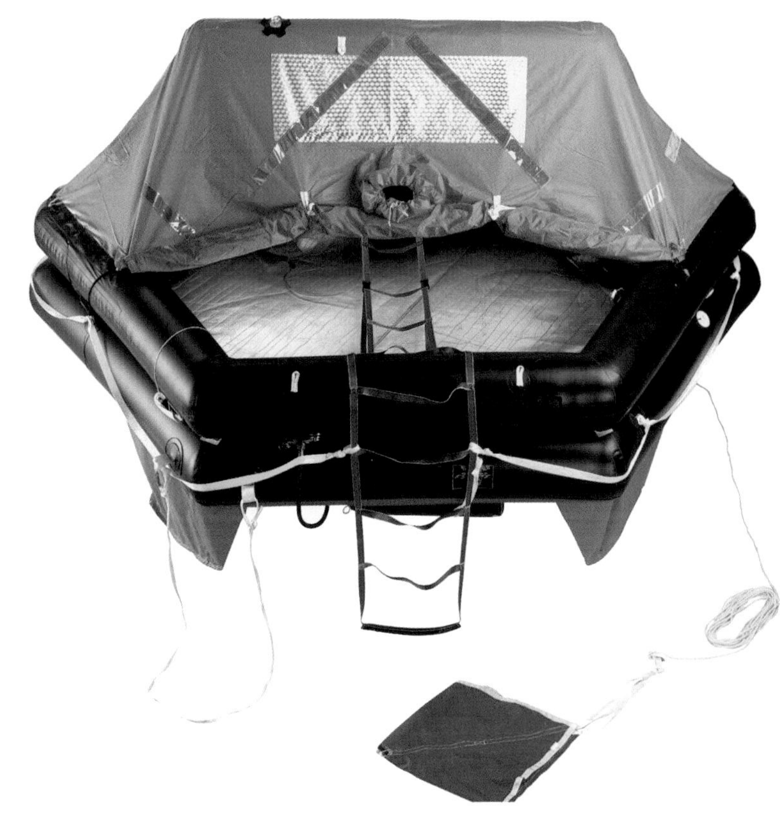

In the 1980s, the engineers at Zodiac came up with the idea of a vacuum-packed life raft in a plastic packet that could be carried as easily as a suitcase. It not only saves space, allowing emergency equipment to be stored on the smallest vessel, but also protects the raft against corrosive elements.

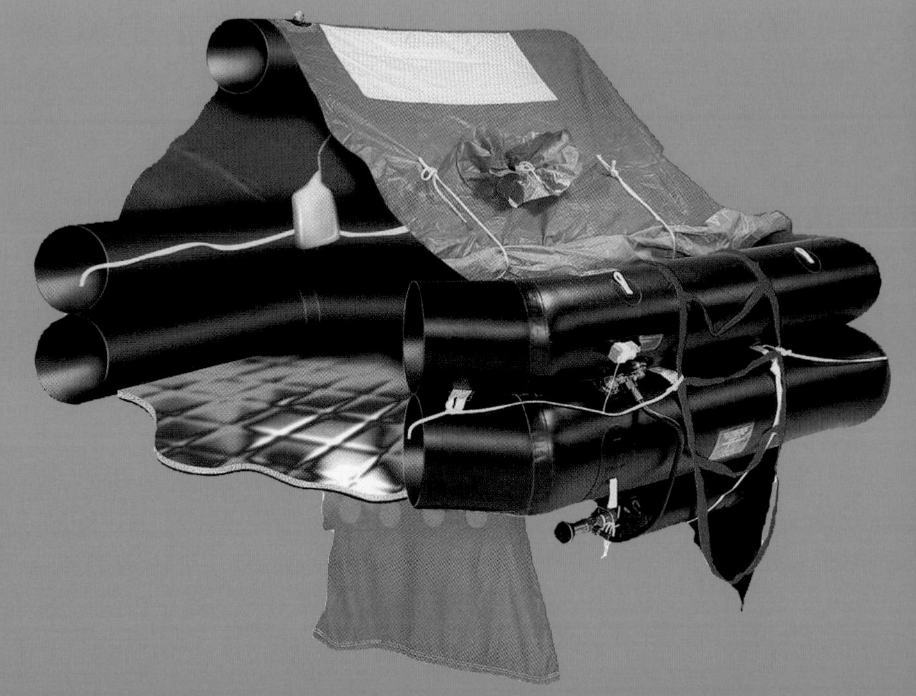

Giancarlo Zema

Jelly-fish 45, Project, 2003

Since the 1950s, flying saucers have captured the collective imagination. Controlled by invaders from some far-off galaxy, they hover over their target and dazzle their victims into confusion with their bright lights. The concept of the floating house by Italian designer Giancarlo Zema features no fewer than three "saucers" that would qualify for a special place in the UFO register. Jelly-fish 45, however, is not based on science fiction, but on the fascinating world of invertebrate marine life.

In an egg-shaped central body with wraparound terraces, the water house can accommodate six people. The steel, glass, and polycarbonate structure is divided into five levels. The underwater observatory with its 360-degree panoramic views lies three meters below the waterline. The daytime rooms, bathroom, kitchen, and promenade deck are just above the waterline while the bedrooms are located on a semi-submerged, intermediate floor. The study room on the upper level echoes the underwater observatory with its own panoramic views at a height of 5.6 meters above the waterline. The Jelly-fish 45 floating house measures fifteen meters in diameter.

The Trilobis 65 houseboat is based on a similar concept. This luxury, twenty-meter yacht has a spacious underwater dome of thermal glass that can be darkened if required. The control room is on the upper level, just above the dining and living area. The sleeping area is at water level, where the movement of the boat is least noticeable. A spiral stairway links the different levels. The body of the boat is strikingly elegant with its overlapping elliptical forms around a central sphere.

With Jelly-fish 45 the Roman designer Giancarlo Zema shows how biomorphic forms can be translated into marine architecture. The result is a floating house with uninterrupted views on five levels, located both above and below the water.

Jelly-fish 45

Giancarlo Zema
Trilobis 65, Project, 2001

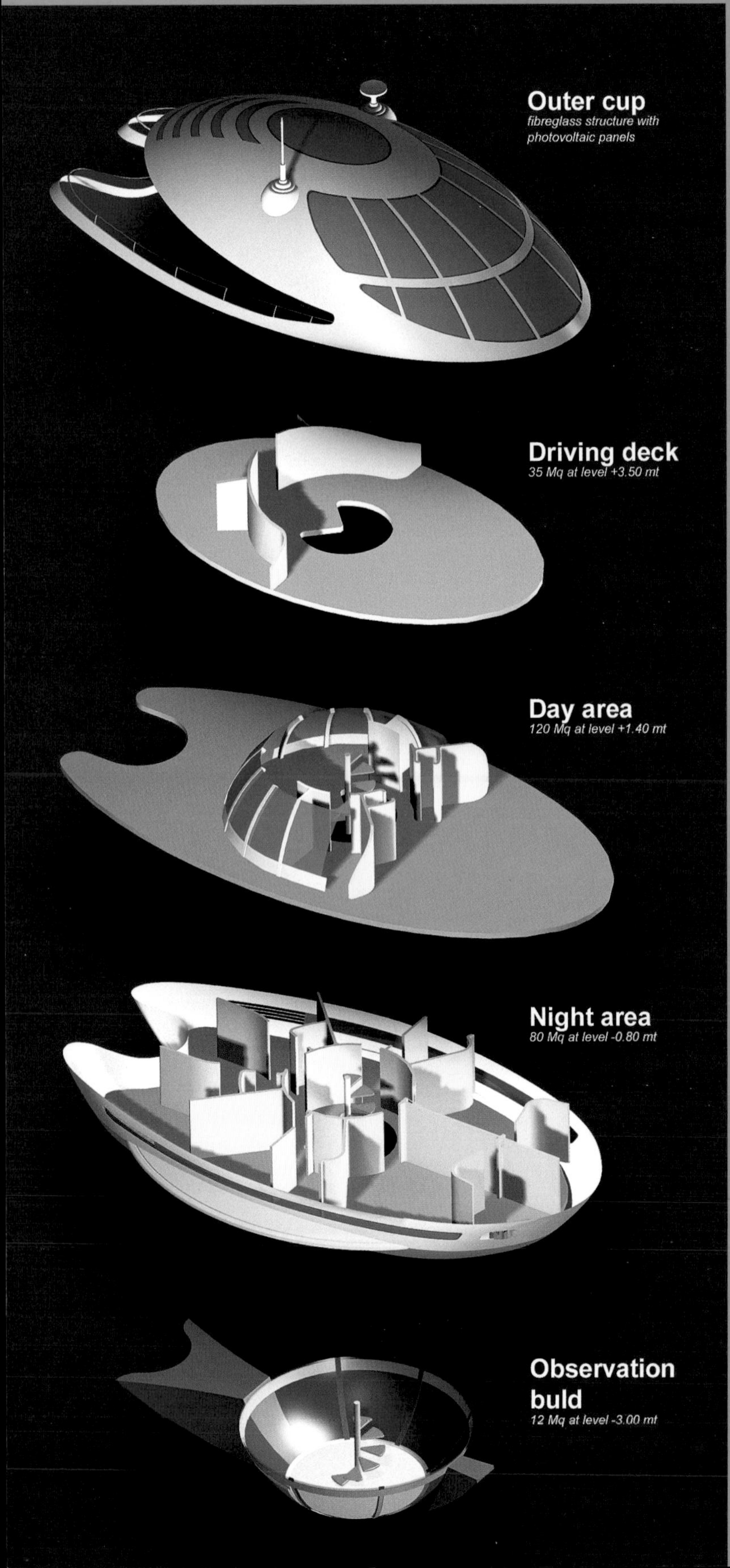

Outer cup
fibreglass structure with photovoltaic panels

Driving deck
35 Mq at level +3.50 mt

Day area
120 Mq at level +1.40 mt

Night area
80 Mq at level -0.80 mt

Observation buld
12 Mq at level -3.00 mt

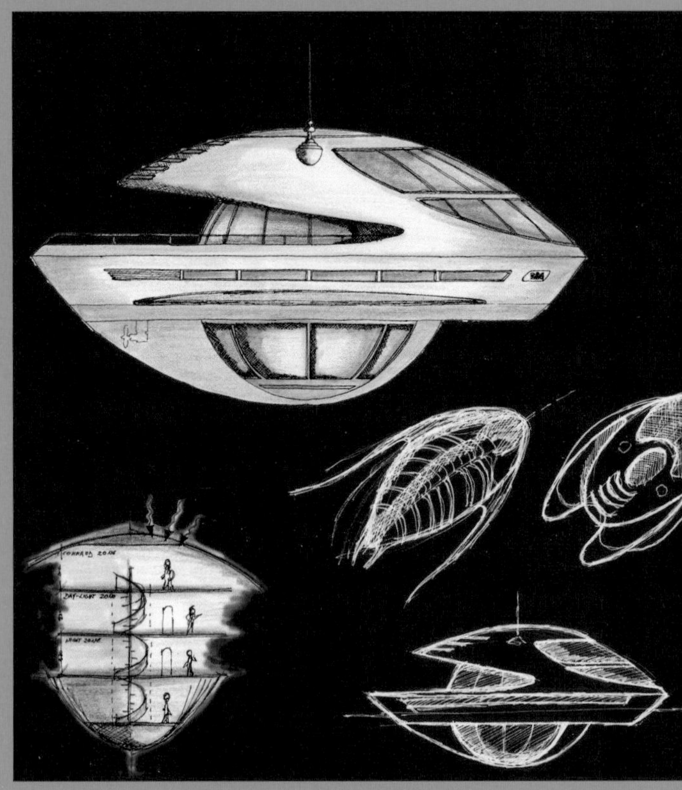

Trilobis is a luxury yacht that looks like an open shell. In spite of having an underwater observatory, the boat is capable of speeds of up to 10 knots. Several Trilobis 65 units can be grouped around a docking station like flower petals.

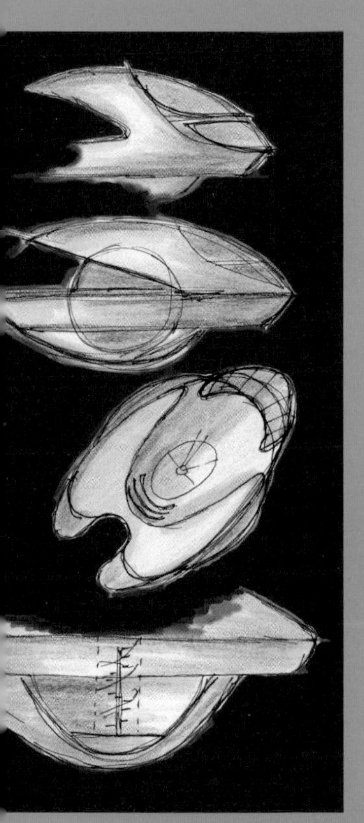

Dirk Schumann

Kamar, No fixed Location, Project, 2002

“Coming Home.” Could an artificial island really be called home? Could people really feel “at home” there, as they would on terra firma? From a distance the water village of Kamar, with its pointed oval dwellings—two sidewalls propped against each other, has a welcoming air. It is only from a bird's-eye view—or from a frog's-eye view—that we see the complexity of the architecture devised by the north-German industrial designer Dirk Schumann, who has succeeded in connecting natural forms with spaceship design asceticism to create a stunning new aesthetic.

These floating islands are in reality conceived as stationary units anchored in sheltered bays and atolls. Each oval platform can hold up to five dwellings, and several modules grouped around a central docking station—which also serves as a helipad—form a larger complex in the shape of an open blossom.

The most important parts of the artificial island, however, are found below the surface of the water. In fact, Kamar has two further functional levels, designed according to very different criteria. On the sloping floor of the sea there is an angular metal and concrete foot, which anchors the island by its sheer weight and connects to it by means of a long tunnel. This underwater tunnel, not unlike the passenger bridges at airports, is a place where people come together, share meals or simply relax and observe the fascinating underwater world through large, semispherical windows.

An important part of Schumann's concept is that the living units should continue underwater so that the sight of the underwater world plays an intrinsic part of everyday life. The floors are provided with sight slits, and a large glass dome—a magnificent viewing space and laboratory combined—ensures that the residents truly feel part of the marine world.

The Kamar project was inspired by the designer's longing to lead an amphibian life on water, and by his awareness that maritime architecture can open up new realms of communication. Even as a child, Schumann was already experimenting with improvised, plastic underwater housing, and he later became a keen diver. Schumann's first design for a diving boat (called Palinurus) was awarded a gold medal in 1997 at the International Design Exhibition in Osaka, which in turn encouraged him to continue work on his dream project.

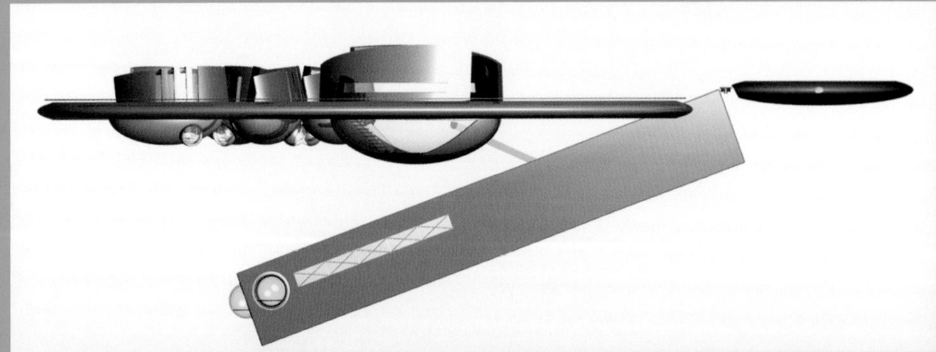

The fascination of Kamar lies both in the overall concept and in its unusual aesthetic. Rather than being motorized, this artificial island is anchored in a sheltered bay. The anchor is partly an inhabitable substructure, and the living areas are all below the surface of the water.

Dirk Schumann
Kamar, No fixed Location, Project, 2002

The island of Kamar is anchored to the seabed by a steel and concrete jetty. This elongated block can be used as a social meeting place with seating areas in the hemispherical portholes that are designed to adjust to the horizontal.

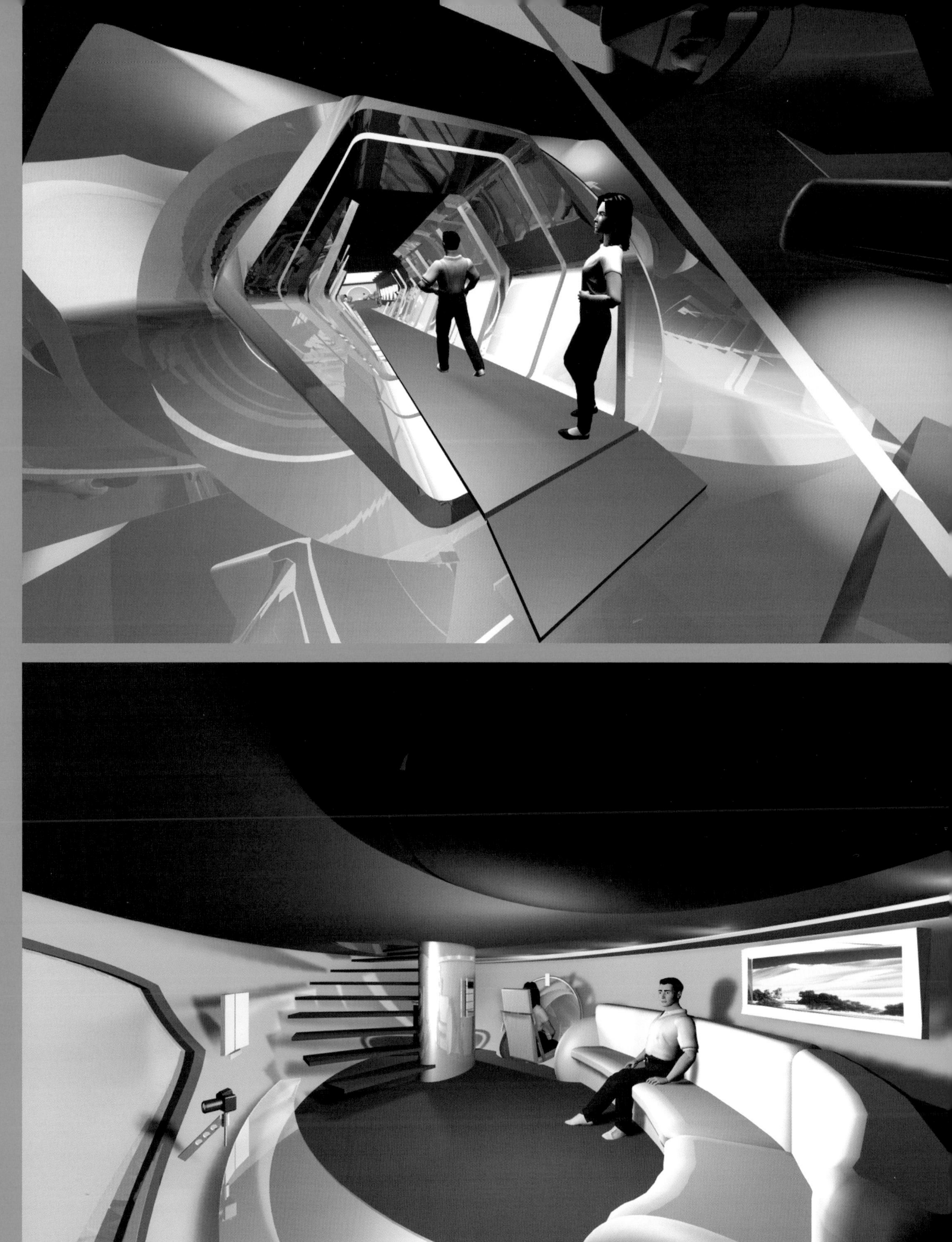

Softroom

Floating Retreat, Project, 1997

The Softroom group's CAD-supported design for a futuristic island, the Floating Retreat, was presented in *Wallpaper* magazine in 1997. According to architects Oliver Salway, Christopher Bagot, and Daniel Evans, they were inspired by land art and packaging artist Christo as well as by NASA moon-landing technology.

One of these days, the only way to find peace and quiet away from the maddening crowds will be on your own inflatable island at sea. This is the witty idea behind what now appears to be a perfectly feasible design. The Floating Retreat is a kind of floating saucer with a lid, a mega-cabriolet, or a supershell with baldachin that can close and disappear, or unfurl in the middle of an island of polyurethane.

The designers thought of every technical detail. As soon as the roof of the streamlined retreat flips up at the press of a button, a generator inflates the kilometer-long island to form a private bathing lagoon. The emptied hull becomes a fully equipped beach hut—bedroom, living room, and bar—with a sound system and neoprene-upholstered fiberglass furniture. An important challenge was stabilizing and reinforcing the gently downward-sloping edges of the island to withstand wind and waves. Additional stabilizers, anchor, and keel prevent the island from capsizing in stormy seas.

When the retreat is no longer needed, the air is sucked out of the gigantic airbag by built-in fireman's hoses and everything packed away again. The retreat, like a huge whale, can be towed away to another location by motorboat.

This high-tech miracle is not aimed at camping enthusiasts looking for a budget holiday pitching tents and stowing space-saving gadgets, but at jet-setters in search of seclusion and independence in accustomed luxury, all without damaging the environment.

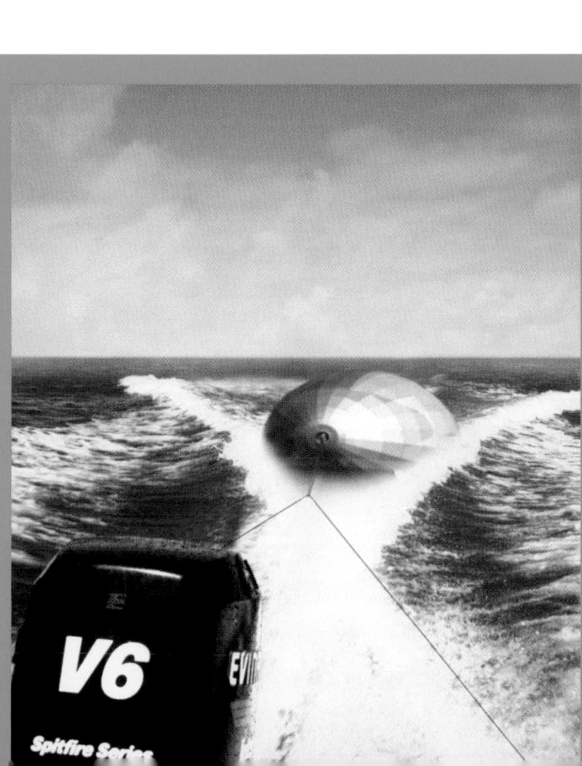

Once it has been towed to its destination, a generator inflates the polyurethane island of the Floating Retreat—while you relax in the little beach house.

Softroom
Floating Retreat, Project, 1997

The private beach lounge is comfortably equipped with bedroom, living room, and bar, complete with neoprene-upholstered fiberglass furniture. The Softroom team has thought of everything that the jet-setter of the future needs for relaxing amid unspoiled scenery.

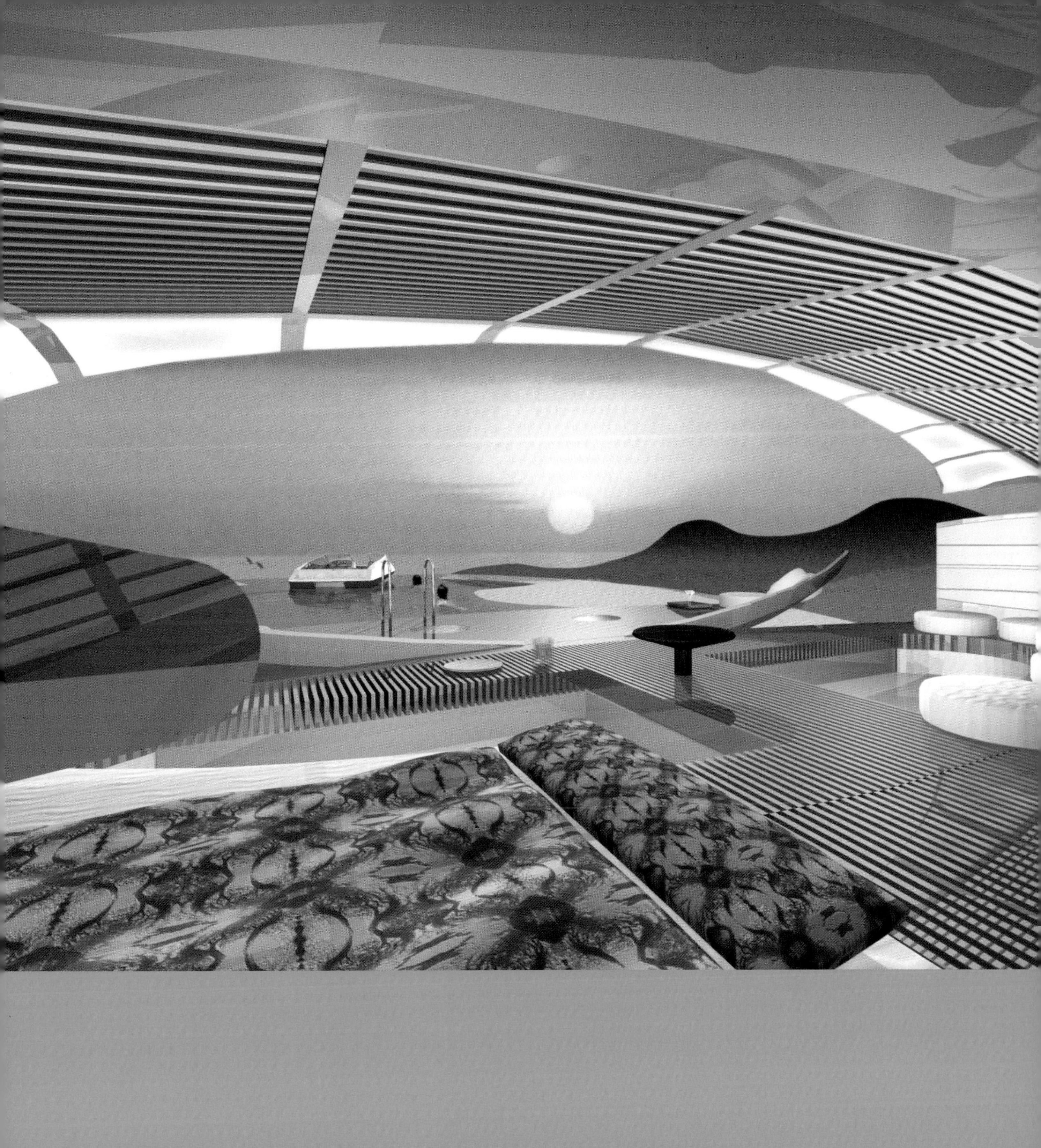

Robert Poff

Sea Venture Hotel, No fixed Location, Project, 2000

The kinds of people who wish to stay at the Sea Venture Hotel get bored hanging around elegant hotel swimming pools—this is a place for indulging in watersports until the sun goes down! At night, guests mingle on the rooftop terrace under the sweeping arc of light that spans the ship from bow to stern.

Sea Venture is no cruise ship for the high seas. Even though it does have a diesel engine, this is a stationary ship hotel designed for sheltered bays. What sets it apart from an onshore hotel is the fact that each of the twelve suites has its very own beachfront. The Caribbean Model even has the unique feature of a maisonette apartment with one level above the waterline and one below, linked by a spiral staircase. Below the waterline is a cozy en suite cabin with a panorama window affording fascinating views of the underwater world and the play of light in the water.

The Sea Venture concept envisions the ship as complementary to onshore hotels, rather than as a substitute—watersport enthusiasts and families can book a beachfront apartment by the day.

There are two varieties of Sea Venture Hotels. The conventional model offers simple hotel rooms with beachfront. The Caribbean model has apartments with underwater cabins.

Kiyonori Kikutake

Marine City, Open Sea, South of Tokyo and Yokohama, Japan, Project, 1958–1963
Aquapolis, Okinawa, Japan, 1975
Linear Marine City, Between Osaka and Kyushu, Japan, Project, 1990

In the 1950s, the Japanese architect Kiyonori Kikutake propagated "land for man to live, sea for machine to function" and designed floating factories as a solution to the labyrinthine density of Japan's metropolitan areas. A founding member of the Metabolists—a futuristic movement of young Japanese architects formed in Tokyo in 1960—he called for urban planning concepts that could keep pace with social change. Finding these aims incompatible with the historic urban structures of land-based cities, Kikutake concentrated on planning full-scale complexes for living and working on water.

Kikutake presented his first designs for a floating industrial complex at a 1958 congress on modern architecture in the Netherlands: six saucer-shaped islands four kilometers in diameter float like water lilies with curled-up rims on the open sea. The production plant—Kikutake had in mind a largely automated chemicals factory—is housed in the cylinders that burrow downwards from the platforms like huge mine shafts. In the years following, Kikutake refashioned the industrial islands as city islands with apartment cylinders rising upwards.

One of the few marine projects by Kikutake to actually have been built is the floating exhibition pavilion Aquapolis for the 1975 International Ocean Exposition in Okinawa. Consisting of massive hollow columns supporting the deck and the exhibition space below, the Aquapolis was built in Hiroshima and later towed to Okinawa in seven days. This prototype floating city was dismantled in the year 2000 due to rust damage and scrapped by an American company.

Kikutake's most radical design is a linear floating city forming a 400-kilometer link between the city of Osaka and the island of Kyushu. This ribbon-like city, cutting through the Inland Sea, is intended to take the pressure off the densely populated coastal area of seven million inhabitants, largely blighted by industrial complexes. The marine city concept also has other obvious advantages. The layout can be altered quite easily. Modules with schools can be linked with, say, sports centers, and later, if necessary, docked on to another area such as a residential zone. The linear plan not only facilitates such alterations, but also permits rapid transport links between all parts of the city—a magnet train could travel the entire length of the city within an hour.

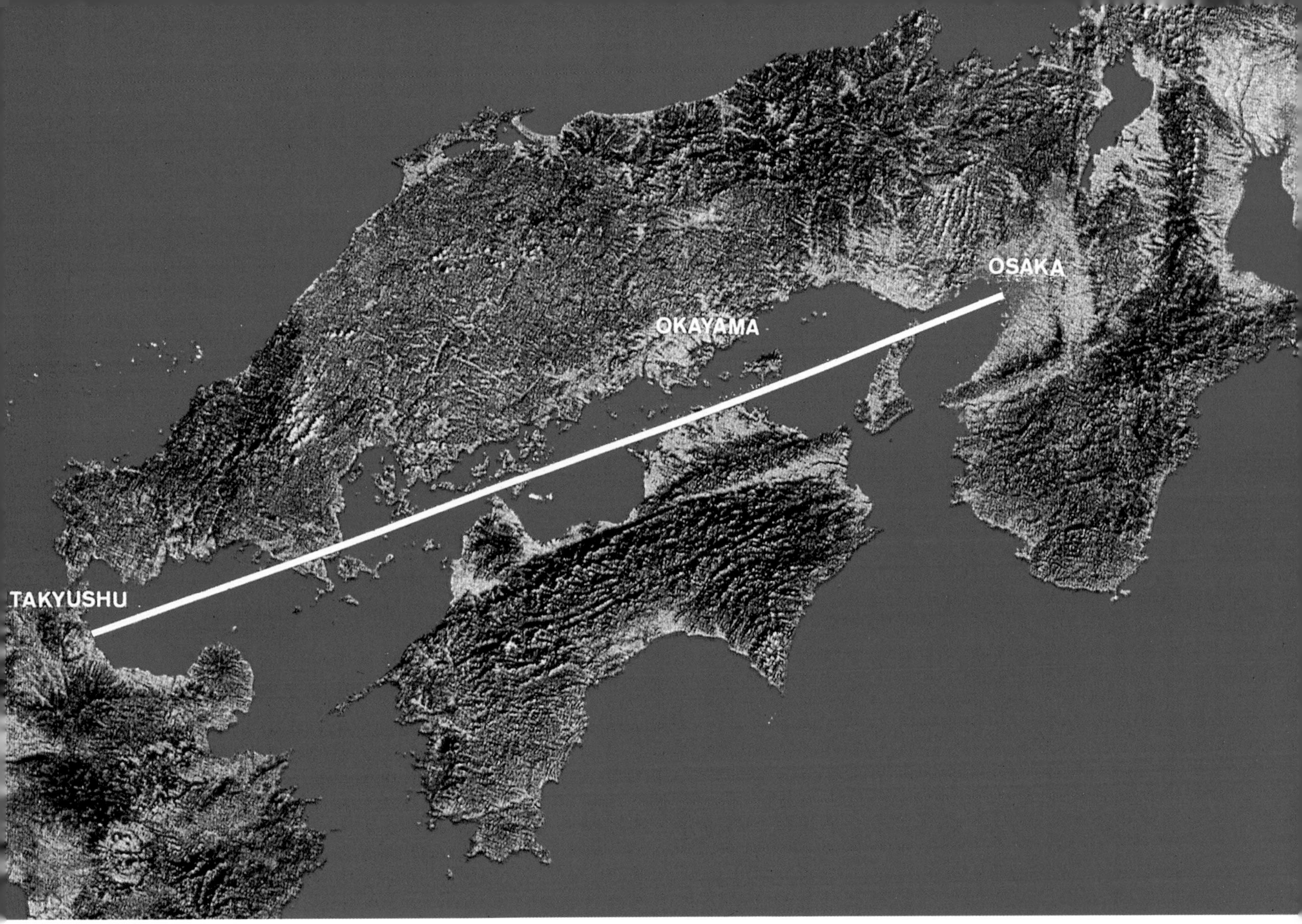

OSAKA

OKAYAMA

TAKYUSHU

Kikutake's designs for marine cities have become highly topical in the 21st century. The linear Marine City design is composed of units for living, working, and cultural activities, which are set together in one straight line connecting Osaka and the island of Kyushu. Aquapolis (opposite page, left, and middle), 120 meters squared, is the first marine urban structure ever realized. Kikutake's circular Marine City design (opposite page, right) envisions a floating city with high-rise buildings.

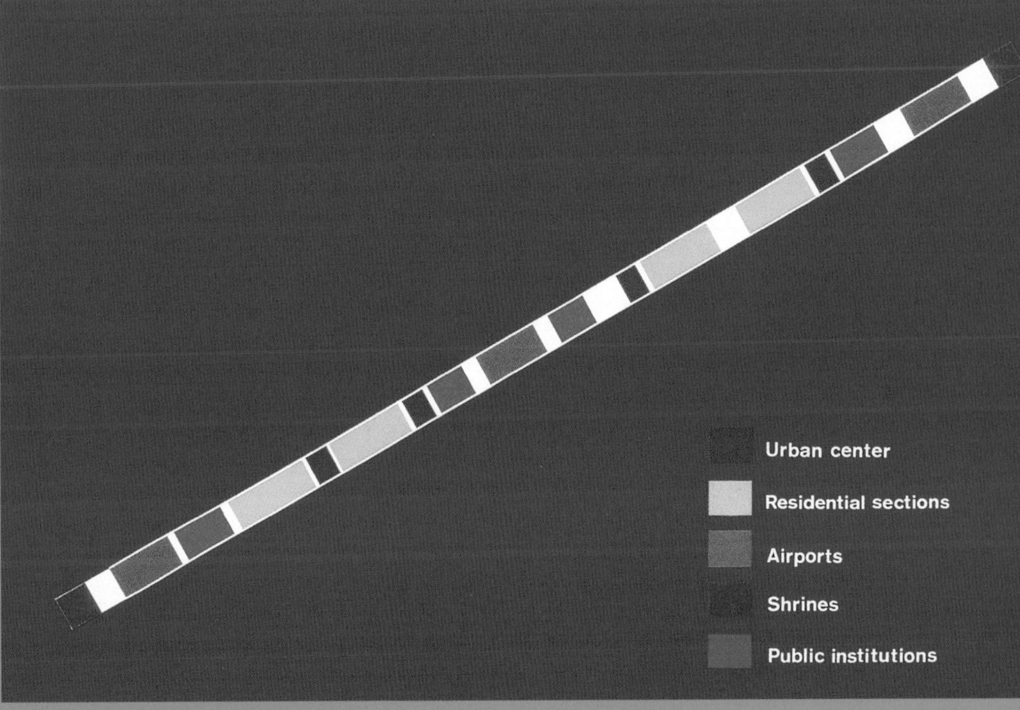

Jean Philippe Zoppini

AZ Island, Project, 2002

A city goes travelling. AZ Island, the floating universe designed by Jean Philippe Zoppini, looks set to become reality. His vision of a utopian island plying the seas like a gigantic ship seems to bring our yearning for boundless freedom and mobility within reach, albeit on an almost surreal scale. The egg-shaped structure that stands fifteen stories above the water offers short-stay guests and permanent residents luxurious and secure accommodation for months or years. This is no luxury cruise liner with the usual array of concert halls, cinemas, theatres, ballrooms, bars, restaurants, shopping malls, and gyms. The architect has thought far further than that to come up with the ultimate in achievable quality of life, hampered so far only by the lack of necessary funding. There was a time when architecture served first and foremost to provide shelter from the elements. Today, it seems that architecture seeks to surpass nature itself.

This floating city carries its own island complete with lagoon. It has beaches, gardens, sports stadiums, and parks as well as two large docks with jetties for residents' and visitors' boats and an attractive marina. Couch potato meets globetrotter in this world of stationary mobility measuring three hundred by four hundred meters in size. In this artificial paradise of metal, constructed of easy-to-assemble modules, you can circumnavigate the globe in three years at a speed of ten knots without ever having to leave the comfort of your home.

Needless to say, the safety of the residents has been given as much thought as the smooth-running infrastructure. In the event of an emergency occurring in spite of all the security measures taken, there are two helicopters and fifty lifeboats available.

If the dream came true, people could circumnavigate the globe in three years in this floating city. Supply ships could unload all that is needed for the ten thousand inhabitants in the city's own port.

Norman Nixon

Freedom Ship, Project, 2000

Towards the end of the nineteenth century, Jules Verne dreamt of the boundless possibilities of a machine world in his techno-utopian novels. In the novel *Propeller Island* he describes a floating city of steel called Milliard City that is a paradise for millionaire tax exiles. The island has boulevards flanked by magnificent villas and palatial offices. It has concert halls, a theater, an observatory, houses made of aluminum, and a transport system that is a cross between a tram and a high-speed train. Three-quarters of the island are given over to agriculture. Residents feel as if they are on the mainland.

The visionary Milliard City of the 21st century is the Freedom Ship designed by the Florida-based engineering group Freedom Ship International. This ship designed for living, working, and recreation looks like an oversized aircraft carrier. The project has all the trappings of a luxury cruise ship and even has parks designed by landscape architects, complete with artificial waterfalls. The eighteen thousand living units can accommodate a population of forty thousand from different income brackets, as well as a twenty thousand-strong crew. As in any city of this size, there is a hospital, schools, sports facilities, and a transport system. The ship's income is ensured by a casino, hotels with a capacity for up to ten thousand guests a day, and thirty thousand tourists visiting the tax-free shopping malls. The ship will cruise slowly around the world, anchoring near the coast of picturesque and economically wealthy areas.

The ship's construction is based on conventional technology. The lightweight superstructures will be mounted on a huge barge equipped with engines and power generators. A two thousand-strong security staff will be in charge of safety on the Freedom Ship. Major feasibility studies and cost analyses have been undertaken and there is already a website on which a wide and varied international community of interested parties from all walks of life is discussing the project.

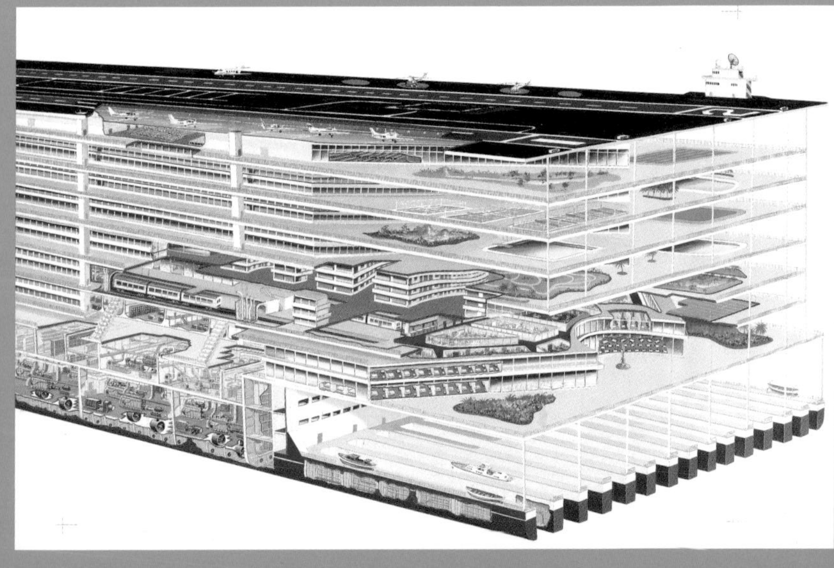

Freedom Ship brings the dream of a floating city within reach. The project combines pragmatic financial and economic considerations with the ideal of an international community and the lure of an adventurous life at sea. The ship will not be an independent state, but will fly under the flag of a country which has yet to be decided. As on any ship, the captain will also have judicial powers.

What could be more natural than to proceed from floating to diving? Life under water with its unmistakable light, its scarcely imaginable wealth of flora and fauna, and its utterly different soundscapes is a world all of its own. Even if the at-times-gigantic visions of the 1970s have not been realized, the under-water world persists as an inviting, challenging realm for mankind to explore and inhabit.
At the beginning of the 21st century this has turned into a competition which inspires engineers, architects and entrepreneurs alike. Underwater refuges present a challenge to individualists with a taste for adventure and exploration and having a meal in an underwater restaurant while fish gaze in at us is already a reality. And what was dismissed as science fiction until very recently may well become a concrete reality in the coming years —an under-water five-star hotel.

Submerging Architecture

1 2 **3** 4

Jacques Rougerie

Galathée, France, 1976–77
Aquabulle, France, 1977
Aquascope, 1979–1981

When diving, pressure doubles every ten meters. One of the biggest challenges in underwater habitats and aquatechnology is countering this pressure and protecting the system against the ingress of water. Marine flora have dealt with the same problems by developing, over the millennia, life forms more perfectly adapted to their environment than that of any land-based plants or animals.

The underwater stations designed by French underwater explorer and aquatic architect Jacques Rougerie are based on his close study of these natural forms. Even the way an air bubble behaves under water, according to Rougerie, demonstrates complex systems that can be adopted in technology: "A simple bubble, a perfect pearl of air, can resist incredible pressure and take all types of form." Indeed, one of Rougerie's early projects, his underwater observatory Aquabulle developed in 1977 and in production since 1978, is reminiscent of an enormous bubble. The spherical room for two divers consists of two plastic shells pressed together by the water pressure. It is accessed through an aperture in the floor. Ballast is attached to a simple frame to stabilize the structure in the water.

The semi-mobile, underwater station Galathée, developed by Rougerie in 1976, is capable of diving to depths of forty-five meters. Its squid-like form with spherical portholes and a decompression chamber has a ballast buoy integrated into its conical base, allowing the research station to retain its position at any given depth.

Rougerie has developed several innovative trimarans. Their common characteristic is a keel construction turned into an observatory for several people to watch the underwater sourrounding through huge, circular portholes. The fantastic looking Aquascope is still being used today.

Jacques Rougerie's own home, aptly enough, is not on land, but in water. He lives on a houseboat—a converted barge—on the Seine in Paris. The unremarkable exterior conceals an interior that is already the stuff of legend, in which utopian dreams have become reality. Sturgeons swim in the "house garden" and there is even a spherical aquarium where children can swim and dive. He has a car for excursions into the surrounding area—but, needless to say, he can also use it to take short cuts through the water, for it is an amphibious vehicle.

Aquascope is an underwater observatory trimaran offering up to eight people the possibility to discover subaquatic life (bottom left). When divers want to take a rest they do not have to surface but can relax underwater in the life balloon Aquabulle (bottom middle). The squid-like underwater observatory Galathée is a habitat offering living facilities to scientists (top right). Rougerie's boat house is a marvel of aquatic home architecture with a spherical aquarium where you can swim together with sturgeons (top left). For excursions an amphibian car can be used.

Dirk Schumann

Palinurus, Project, 1997–2003

It may move in the water, but that is about the only thing that German industrial designer Dirk Shumann's visionary concept has in common with a ship. The visible part of the Palinurus submarine extends one meter out of the water, like an oversized periscope or the head of some mythical sea creature. One meter below the surface, the large, streamlined oval section—made of heavy materials and acting as a stabilizing keel—houses the living and sleeping areas, a library, and service facilities. Models were built to test the structure and side stabilizers were mounted to balance it out. The structure is able to compensate for minor wave movements, thereby creating two stable areas, one above water and one below.

Schumann presented the first Palinurus model in Japan in 1997 and was awarded the prestigious Golden Prize of the Japanese Design Foundation. In this prototype, Schumann developed the concept of the keel as a functional space in the form of a glass sphere with seating for panoramic views. The latest version has an underwater cabin for five to six people and is 13.4 meters long by 8.5 meters wide. The glass capsule is located at the front and allows residents to feel part of the marine life, as there is no visible barrier between the interior and exterior worlds. A transit area in the connecting tower leads to the above-water section with its special diving facilities. The concept now also includes a full-scale service station, for use in sheltered bays as a maintenance dry dock.

The Palinurus project is being further developed by Architectura Navalis in collaboration with various university institutes. Compromise is inevitable in the interests of feasibility; whereas the first design did not envisage any form of propulsion, in the interests of a more sensitive approach to nature, the later designs have engines.

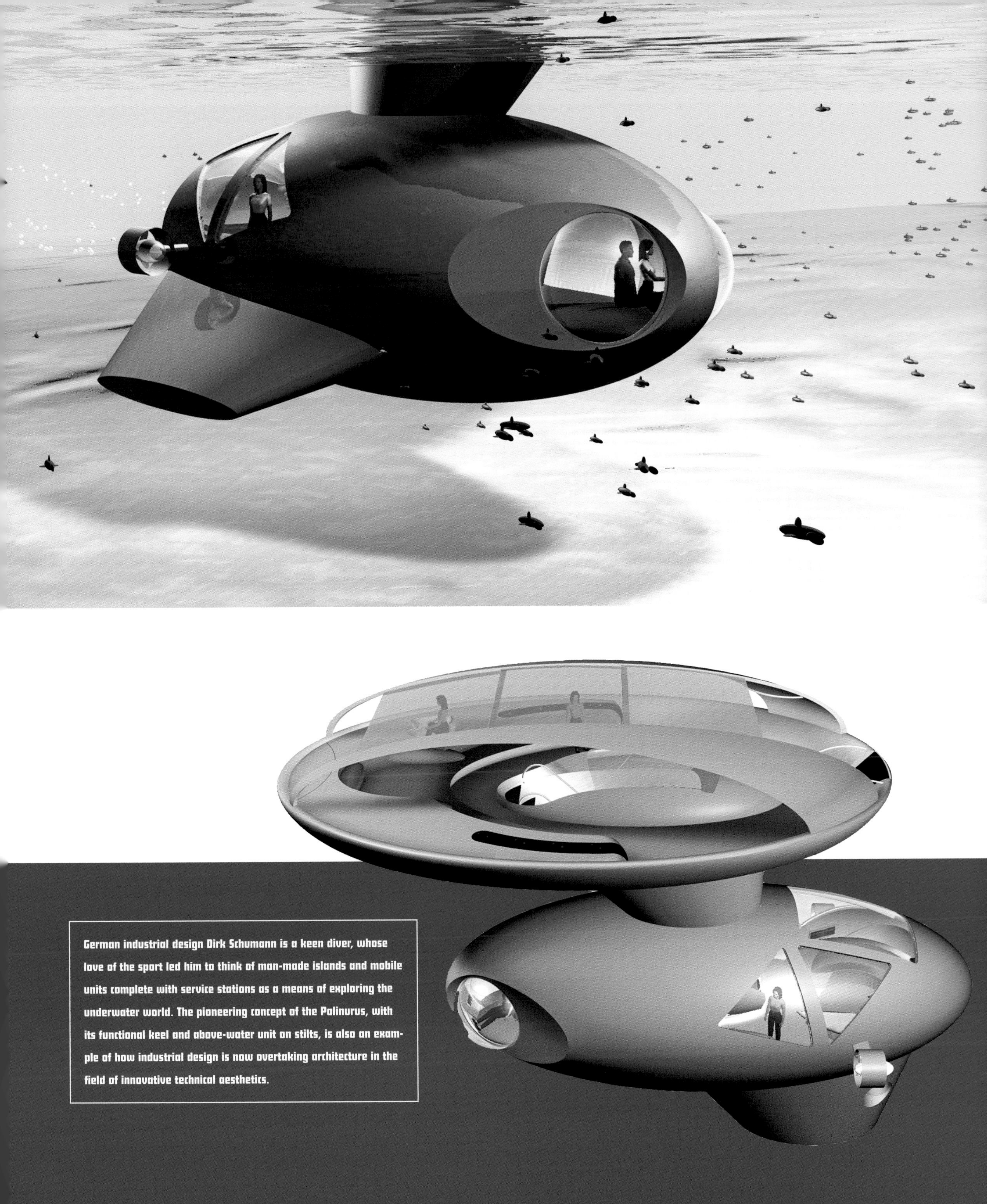

German industrial design Dirk Schumann is a keen diver, whose love of the sport led him to think of man-made islands and mobile units complete with service stations as a means of exploring the underwater world. The pioneering concept of the Palinurus, with its functional keel and above-water unit on stilts, is also an example of how industrial design is now overtaking architecture in the field of innovative technical aesthetics.

tools off.architecture

underwater retreat, Project, Since 2003

City life is often stressful. What an appealing idea to withdraw to an underwater retreat to find some peace and quiet. The Munich-based architects Eva Durant and Andreas Notter sought to create a place of contemplation and meditation. The organically formed polycarbonate structure houses a whole new world. At the entrance aperture there is a little elevator that takes the guest under water. The sounds of the outside world fall silent and the temperature plummets as the ground gradually nears. The cozy little living area has furniture sunk into the floor to free up the 360-degree view. Even the technical fittings are installed under the floor, which is designed as a large shell. The huge sunken bathtub, which provides uninterrupted underwater views, is a real highlight. It would be easy to spend an entire weekend in such a retreat.

The underwater retreats are fronted by floating wooden verandas. The pontoon structure is accessed by boat from the mainland. The open spaces are intended for water sports and sunbathing and form a self-contained unit with the secluded underwater room.

Construction is to be undertaken in dry dock and the completed houses towed to their destination, where the living area is then sunk about seven meters below the waterline and stabilized by three steel cables attached to the foundations.

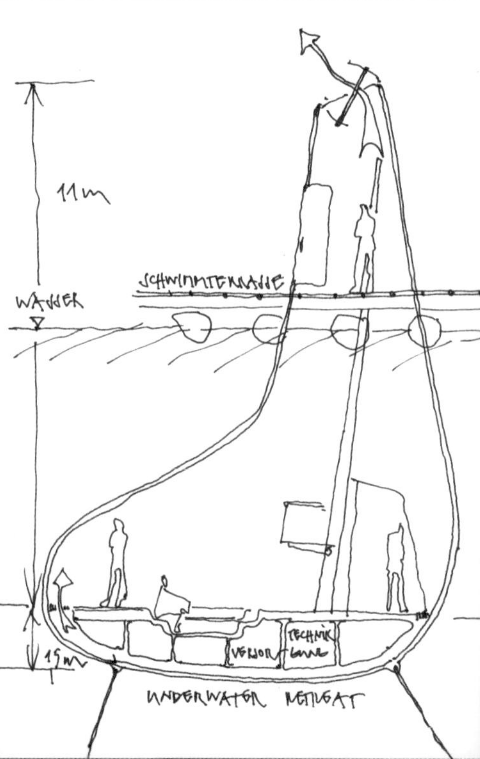

In the architects' office there is a model of the underwater retreat floating in a large aquarium full of brightly-colored fish. The pictures show how this small, one-room underwater world might look. Almost all the fittings and fixtures, including a bathtub, are integrated into the floor shell to provide breathtaking 360-degree views.

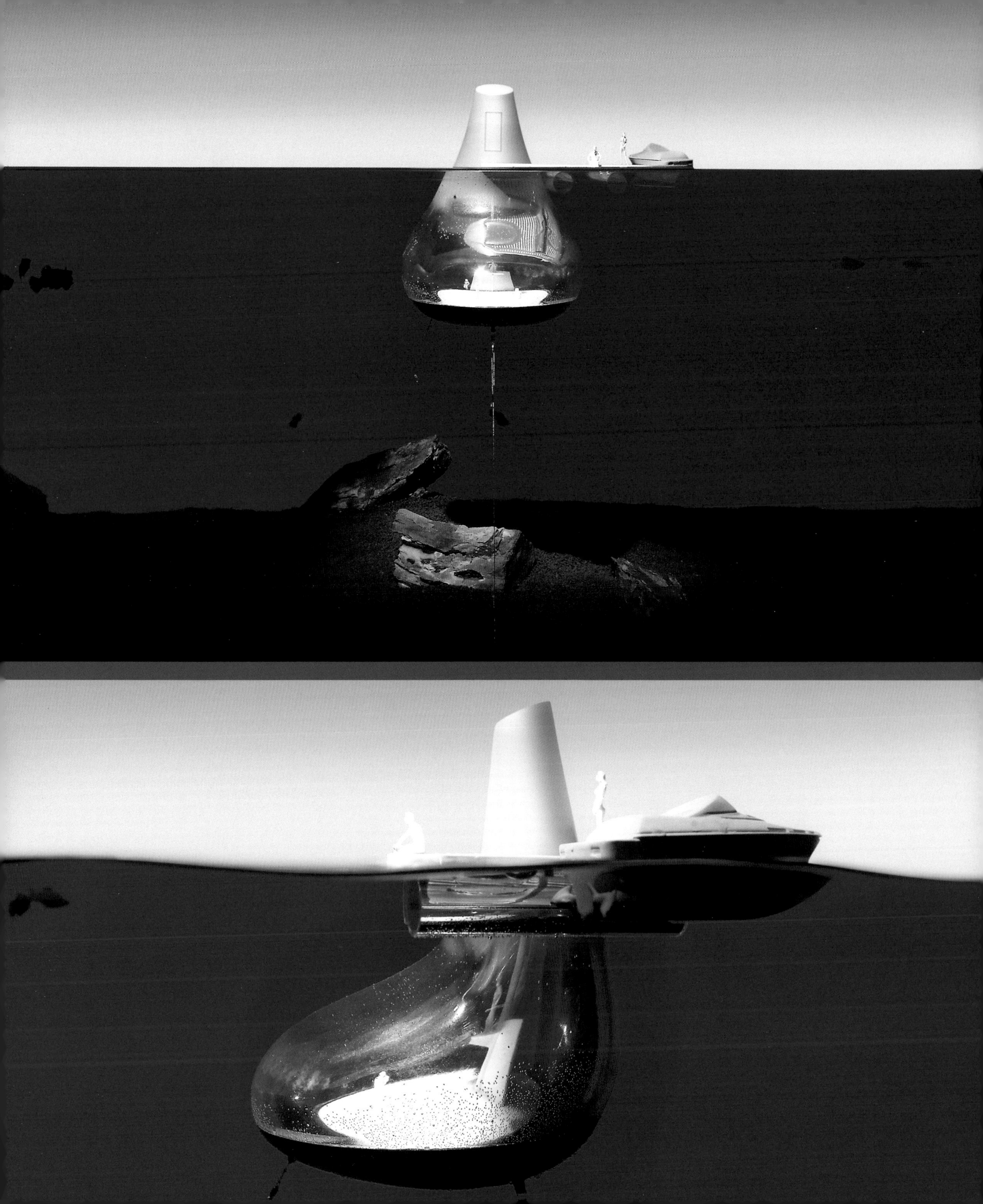

Ian Koblick and Neil Monney

Jules' Undersea Lodge, Key Largo, Florida, USA, Since 1985

Anyone booking a weekend in the Undersea Lodge has to have a sense of adventure and a pioneering spirit, because this former deep-sea marine research laboratory converted into a miniature hotel lies on a lagoon bed seven meters below the waterline and can only be reached diving. Scuba diving novices have to take a short course of instruction. Thus prepared, guests can make their way, with no luggage, to their underwater accommodation. It stands on stilts, and is accessed from below through the so-called "moon pool" that forms the entrance to the Undersea Lodge. "It's like discovering a secret underwater clubhouse," say project developers Ian Koblick and Neil Monney.

A maximum of six people can stay in this tiny lodge with just two cabins and a living room. Though the rooms themselves are small, there is a huge porthole with a fabulous view of the underwater world. Angelfish, parrot fish, barracudas, and snappers peek through the window and gaze in wonder at the guests. The lodge is situated in a natural reef fish nursery. The research capsule, which is pressurized to prevent the ingress of water, is equipped with hot showers and a kitchen for gourmet meals. If you don't want to cook, you can order a meal, which is delivered in a watertight package by a diver.

During the day, guests can explore the water anemones, sponges, and oysters of the mangrove bay equipped with unlimited oxygen supplies.

In 1995, a discussion was arranged between Undersea Lodge aquanauts and Space Shuttle astronauts about the similarities between their experiences in "outer space" and "inner space," neither of which bears any comparison to living on land.

When the La Chalupa continental shelf research station off Puerto Rico was decommissioned, marine scientists Ian Koblick and Neil Monney come up with the idea of using it as an undersea cottage. The underwater capsule has become a popular venue for special occasions—such as weddings.

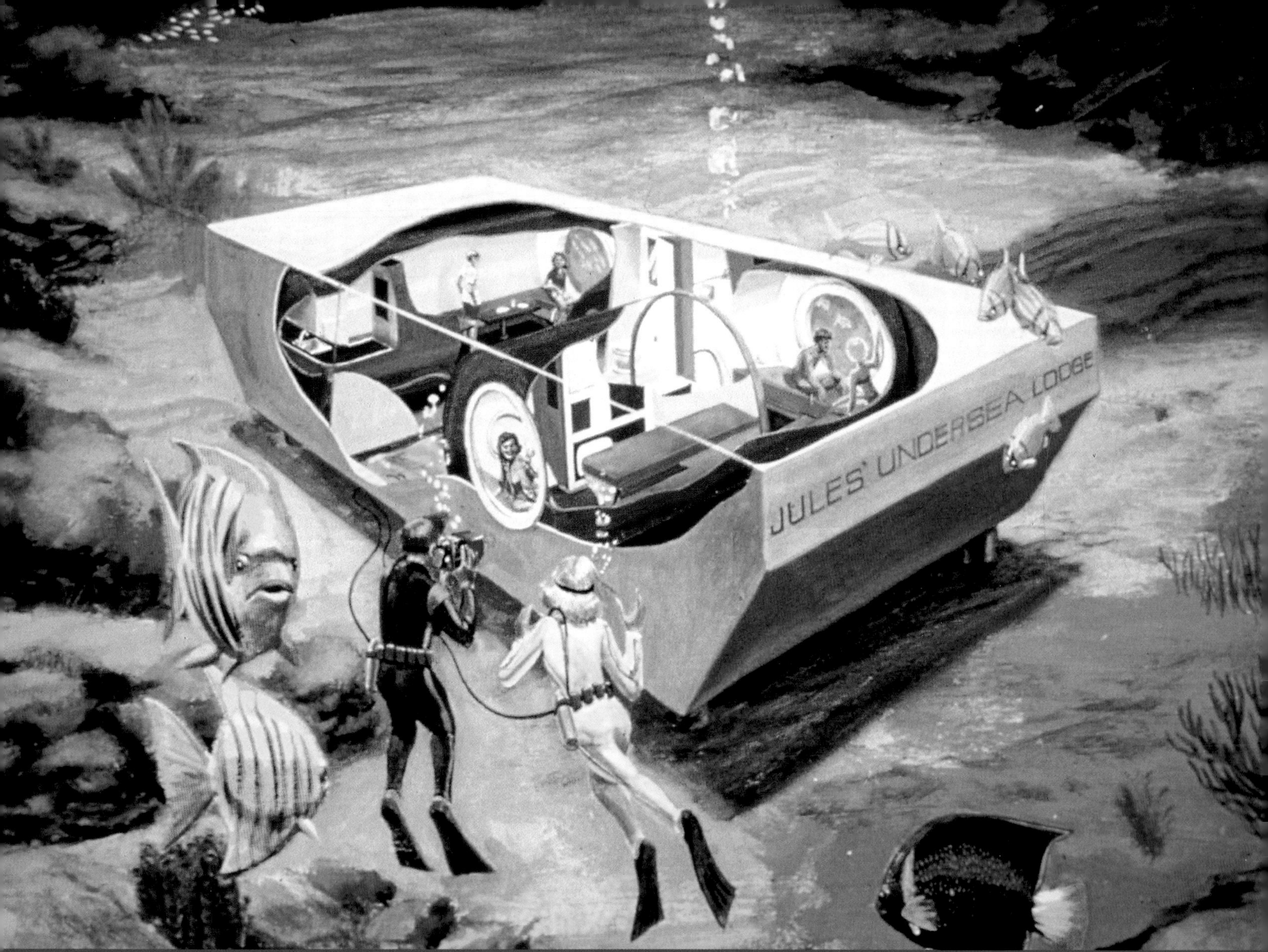

JULES' UNDERSEA LODGE

Joachim Hauser

Hydropolis, Dubai, United Arab Emirates, 2004–2007

From the air the Hydropolis looks like a space capsule floating in the deep blue of the Persian Gulf, tethered to the mainland by a single thread.

As yet the project is still a vision, but the first underwater luxury hotel is scheduled to open as early as 2007. Designed by German architect Joachim Hauser, Hydropolis is being built with support from the government in Dubai. Located 500 meters from the beach at Jumeirah, it promises visitors to this desert state a truly extraterrestrial experience—surrounded by the sea and sky.

Hydropolis—a modern-day "sunken city"—will have two hundred luxurious suites fifteen meters below the surface of the sea. Protected by an artificial, ring-shaped island with a beach and palm groves, the hotel is situated within a "sea lake." The glassed-in hotel rooms—Plexiglas shells up to eighteen centimeters thick—look like huge air bubbles on the floor of the sea. Here guests can retreat into the cool twilight of an underwater world. The suites are connected to a circular corridor, just below the surface of the water and visible at low tide. Tidal movements and changing natural light can thus produce a range of optical effects in the interior of the structure. In addition, the sea lake also contains floating pavilions with a library, smokers' lounge, a quiet area, and leisure islands for women only.

Of course Hydropolis also has all that the city dweller might desire. Below a curved, tubular construction there are shopping streets, conference centers, and cultural venues. The health club and fitness area is equipped with thermal baths in the Roman style. The island is connected to the mainland by a tunnel with special tracks for the two-way transportation modules. The shimmering, fishlike silhouette of the island—bathed by night in cascades of light and multimedia projections—is equal to any of Jules Verne's most fantastic visions.

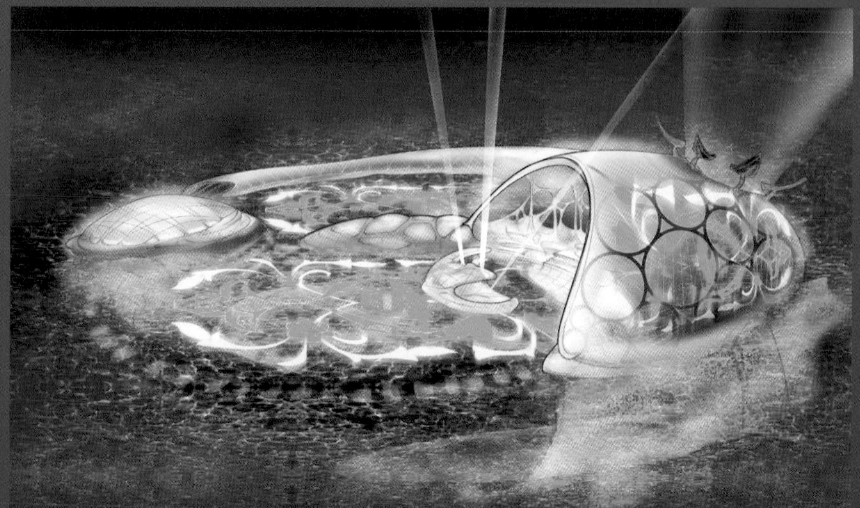

The desert state of Dubai is becoming known for its spectacular hotel complexes that will guarantee its continued prosperity when the oil wells run dry. Scheduled to open in 2007: the first underwater hotel anywhere in the world, designed by the German architect Joachim Hauser.

Sefi Kiryaty and Ayala Serfaty

Red Sea Star, Eilat, Israel, 1995–1999

The underwater world is baroque, sensual, colorful. Scientists and divers have long explored and adored tropical underwater flora, but before the Israeli designer Ayala Serfaty nobody actually came up with the idea of letting the colors and forms of jellyfish, sea cucumbers, sponges, or other water plants inspire an entire interior décor.

In the 1990s, Israeli architect Sefi Kiryaty designed a huge underwater restaurant for the Bay of Eilat in the Red Sea, constructed of steel cells welded in situ and weighed down at six meters below sea level by a concrete plinth. The complex takes the form of a starfish—for practical reasons. This form allows every guest to take a window seat from which to admire the fantastic underwater world of the Red Sea.

Ayala Serfaty had to create an atmospheric interior out of a hollow steel shell. Inspired by the luscious aquatic vegetation, she came up with an organically floral take on Art Nouveau. Acrylic window frames were shaped into underwater forms. Enormous ceiling lamps of pleated silk hover above the tables, spreading a mysterious light. Tentacled stools line the bar that grows out of the floor like a coral reef and columns in the form of sea cucumbers support the ceiling.

As a counterpoint to the bluish aquatic light, the artist chose a warm palette of hues from yellow to orange and red. Otherwise, the blue light from the windows would have affected even the food on the table. And who wants bluish steak and potatoes?

In the Bay of Eilat on the Red Sea an underwater restaurant has been built of steel containers. Israeli designer Ayala Serfaty has created a fantastic interior design based on the forms and colors of aquatic flora. The complex is linked to the mainland by a bridge and accessed by a stairway.

Sefi Kiryaty and Ayala Serfaty
Red Sea Star, Eilat, Israel, 1995–1999

The Red Sea Star gourmet restaurant on the seabed of the Bay of Eilat lies seven meters below the waterline and seats one hundred guests. Have a seaweed salad on a coral table, sit on an anemone barstool, and stare at the starfish lamps through your martini glass.

Richard Buckminster Fuller

Undersea Island, No Location, Patent Granted 1963
Triton City, Tokyo Bay, Project, Early 1960s

The brilliantly innovative American designer and architect Richard Buckminster Fuller was one of the first to explore visionary new concepts of living on land, on water, and under water. Exploring the oceans was, to him, more important than space travel. In the 1950s, long before the first oil crisis, he realized that the industrialized world would soon have to exploit the ocean's resources. With a thoroughly practical bent, he began designing platforms for living and working under water and in 1963 he successfully patented his idea under the evocative name Undersea Island. The patent did not apply to the overall concept, but only to one practical detail: the stable anchorage of a buoyant caisson for living and working under water. This buoyant caisson was designed for the docking of both ships and submarines.

At the same time, Fuller developed the concept of a floating city of low-income housing in Tokyo Bay for a Japanese businessman. The design known as Triton City envisioned individual modules for sixty-five hundred inhabitants, which could be combined to form a larger city. The twenty-story concrete and steel towers were to be assembled in dry dock and towed to their destination. U.S. government studies confirmed the cost analyses and engineering feasibility of Fuller's design.

Buckminster Fuller sought a fundamental pattern in nature on which all biological structures are based, along the lines of the chemical structure of matter. For mainland architecture, he developed the geodesic dome, 300,000 of which have since been built all over the world. His visions of floating cities and underwater platforms for living and working have yet to be realized.

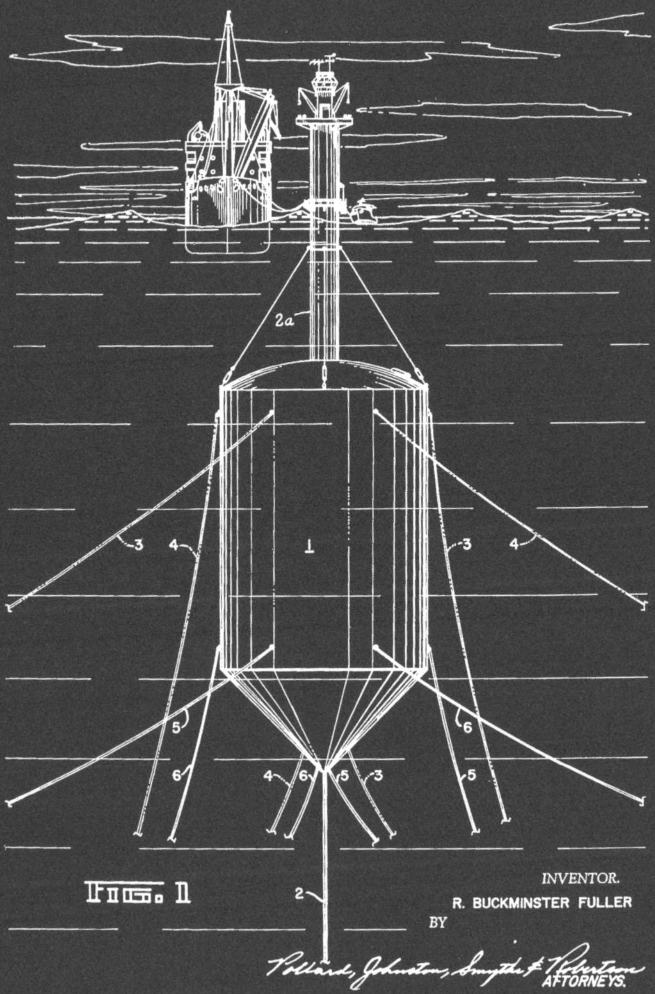

2a
3
4
1
5
6
2
INVENTOR.
R. BUCKMINSTER FULLER
BY
Pollard, Johnston, Smythe & Robertson
ATTORNEYS.

FIG. 1

1a
14
7
11
6a
1
8
2
INVENTOR.
R. BUCKMINSTER FULLER
BY
Pollard, Johnston, Smythe & Robertson
ATTORNEYS.

FIG. 6

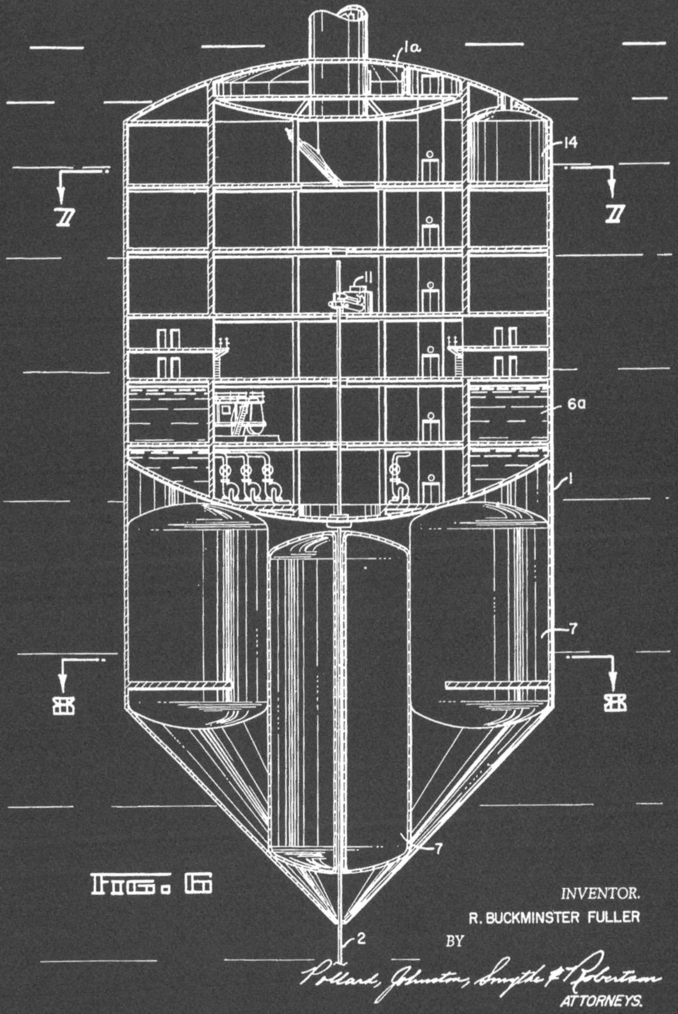

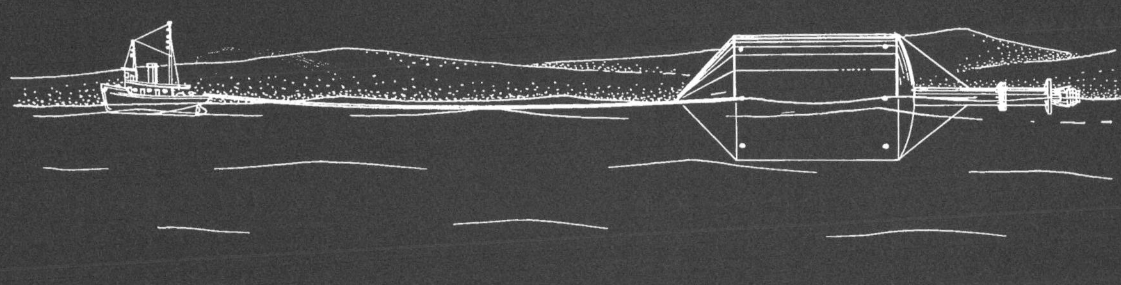

FIG. 13

Drägerwerk AG Lübeck

Helgoland Marine Laboratory, In operation 1969–1980

It hardly bears thinking about: living and working in a nine-meter-long windowless tube just two and one-half meters in diameter, with no outside contact except for radio. For the four aquanauts on board the Helgoland marine laboratory, not even the idealism of being pioneers in the service of science, involved in an important major research project, could prevent the depressing feeling of vegetating in an incapacitated submarine. When the Helgoland marine laboratory was decommissioned in 1980, after operating for a little more than ten years, the conclusion was that "human beings are not suited to staying underwater for lengthy periods without appropriate adaptions. Living permanently on the seabed is also impossible due to serious medical problems."

The project was initially launched by scientists in search of solutions to global overpopulation. At that time, the world's population had passed the three billion mark and was expected to double to six billion by 2003—as indeed it has. The marine laboratory was intended to explore the potential for harnessing the sea's resources to feed the world in the future by establishing deep-sea factories, fish farms, and algae farms on the continental shelf two hundred meters below sea level.

The cramped underwater accommodation was designed for four people. Air, energy, and fresh water were provided via a link to a supply platform. In order to create more space, a pressurized wetroom was added a few years later in which the scientists could prepare for their diving expeditions, with an opening in the floor through which they could leave the laboratory.

Today's possibilities of exploring the sea by means of robots and simulations have made manned marine laboratories obsolete. Nevertheless, this superb feat of technical engineering, on display at the German Maritime Museum in Stralsund since 1998, still bears impressive witness to the pioneering spirit of adventure that prevailed in the age when man first began to explore the ocean depths.

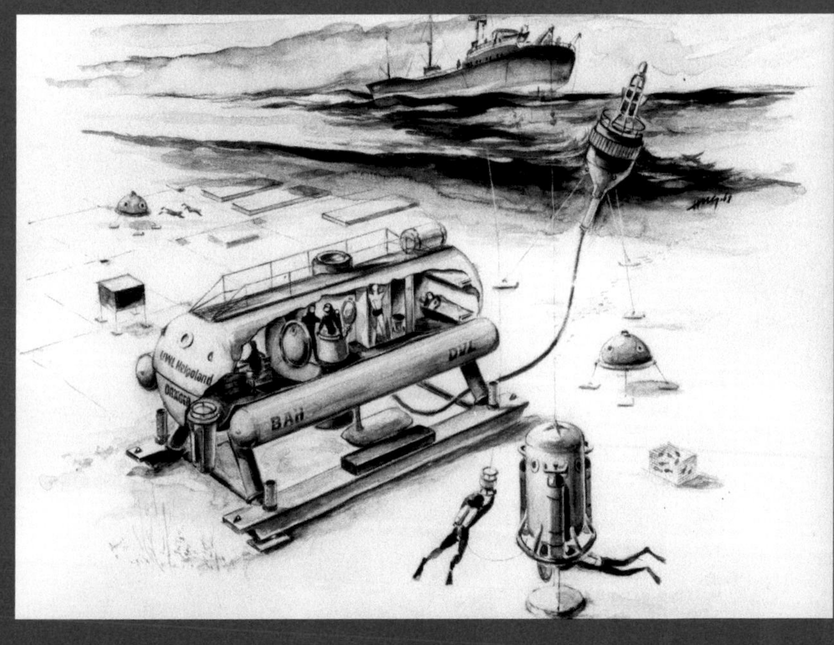

The Helgoland Marine Laboratory was one of a number of visionary missions undertaken in the 1960s, of which the moon landing in 1969 was perhaps the most spectacular. This project was aimed at exploring the possibility of establishing deep-sea farms on the seabed.

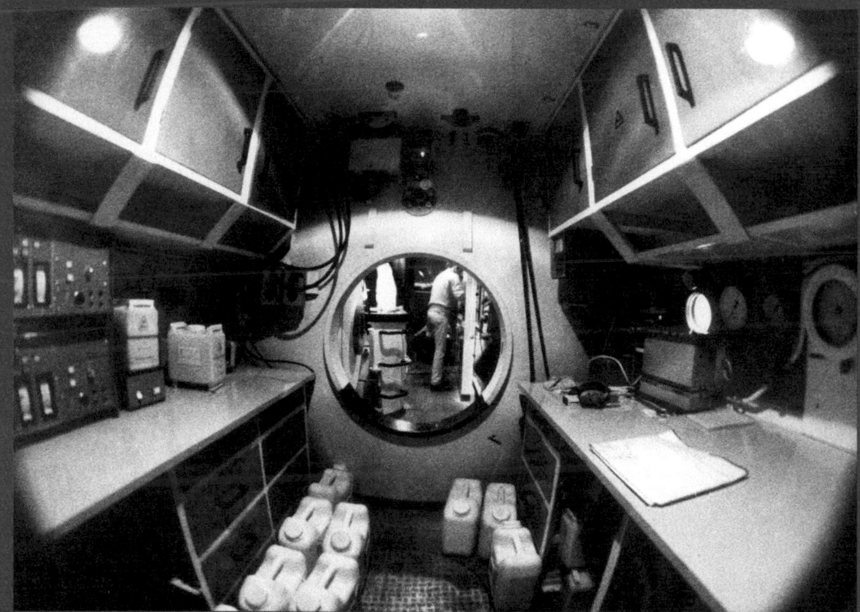

Annette Lippmann, Guido Weinhardt, and Sea & Space GmbH

Seven Oceans One, Project, 2002

For centuries, people have feared the ocean depths. While overcoming gravity and conquering outer space were universal dreams, the underwater world remained the preserve of scientists. This view, however, looks set to change. Having fulfilled the dream of flight in the 20th century, and having made month-long sojourns in space a reality, the race is on in the twenty-first century to explore the possibility of living underwater.

One of the potential winners in this race is the Seven Oceans One project by German architects Annette Lippmann and Guido Weinhardt. The underwater hotel—with accommodation for up to 330 guests—consists of two modules, each 145 meters long and forty-eight meters wide. The buildings are anchored in a fixed steel structure at a depth of ten to twenty meters. This steel structure provides for three levels below the water line and three above. The upper floor forms a promenade twelve meters above sea level, with views of the starry sky unpolluted by urban lights. Its counterpart on the lowest floor, twenty-seven meters below sea level, is a seabed promenade through glass corridors. Excursions in the surrounding waters can be made in a miniature submarine or with diving gear.

A fascinating complex of rooms with extensive glazing allows guests to experience the colorful realms of the underwater world from inside the hotel.

Seven Oceans One is envisioned as an offshore underwater hotel in temperate waters rich in tropical flora and fauna. Its modular structure and dimensions mean that the hotel can be built in a shipyard, and maintenance and repair work carried out in a conventional dry dock.

The prefabricated modules are towed to the chosen site by tugs, the water tanks are flooded to submerge the building to the desired depth, and the structures are firmly anchored in place. Shipbuilding and aviation experts collaborated on the design for this project.

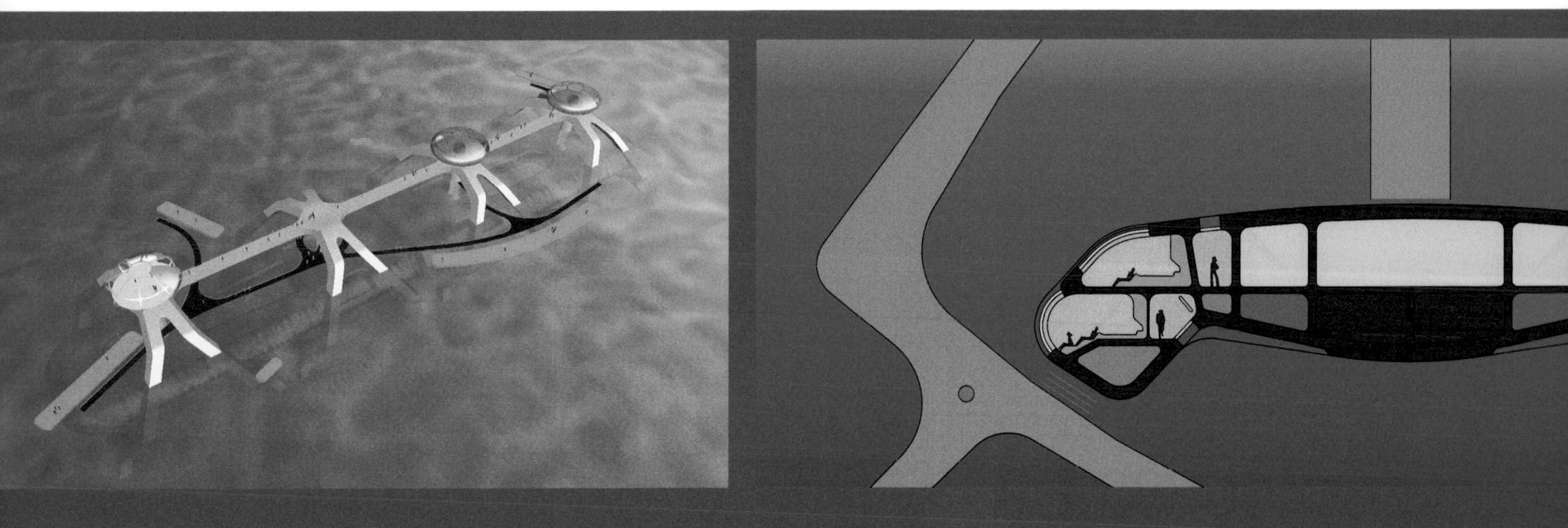

Architects Annette Lippmann and Guido Weinhardt designed Seven Oceans One as a novel hotel experience. Guests arrive by helicopter or boat and enter the silent underwater world by glass elevator. The various decks house all the comforts of a luxury cruise ship, from workout and spa facilities to casino, cinema, and diving station.

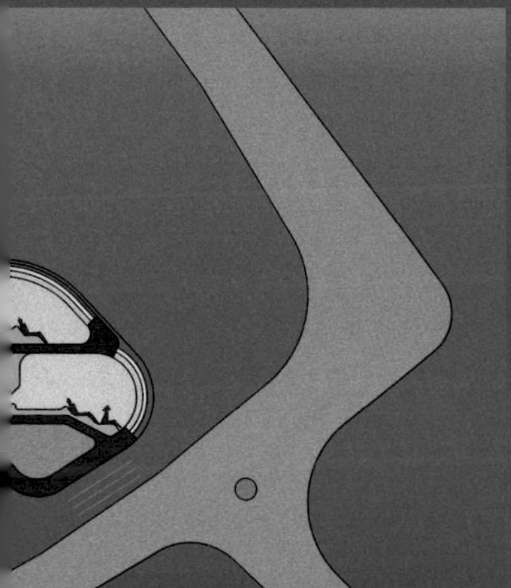

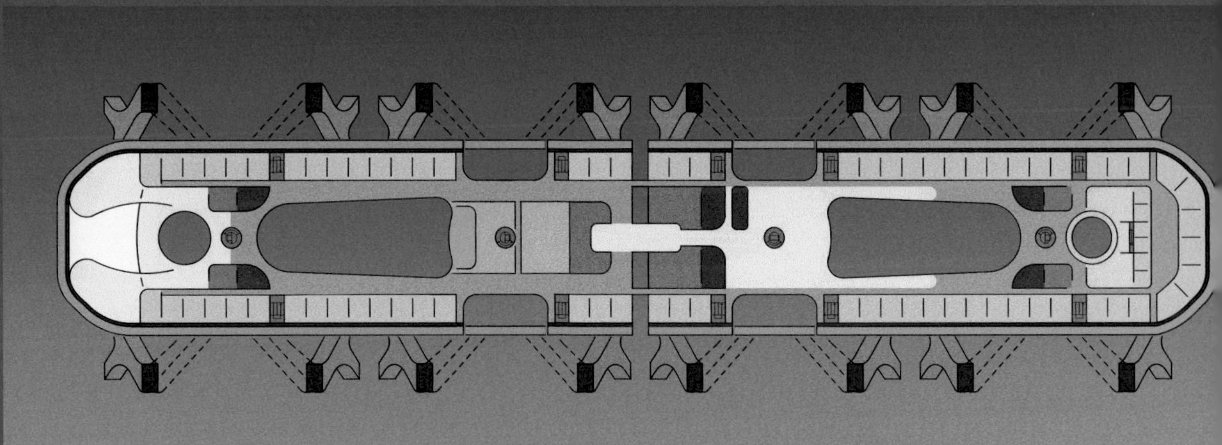

Mikael Genberg

Otter Inn, Lake Mälaren, Västerås, Sweden, 2000

Who has never dreamt of being rocked gently to sleep like a baby? At the Otter Inn that dream comes true. In Sweden's first underwater hotel, guests fall asleep to the gentle movement of the waves and the submarine sounds. The name of the hotel says it all. Like the home of the otter, this unusual accommodation cannot be seen at first glance. Above the waterline there is a raft with a typical red Swedish wooden cabin designed and built by artist Mikael Genberg. Nothing particularly remarkable about that. But the real surprise is below the waterline—a twenty-four-ton watertight tank held by two anchors. The thirteen-square-meter bedroom—with two beds, a table, and four lamps—has panorama windows on all sides offering fantastic views of the underwater world in all its changing colors. At night it is completely dark, and in the daytime the flora and fauna of the lake can be seen in a yellowish-green tint.

A stairway leads up into the little wooden house above the water, where the bathroom and the kitchen—which also serves as the reception area—are located. The electricity supply is solar powered. Guests who book the deluxe version can even have their meals delivered to the remote, one-room hotel. A canoe is provided for forays to the many uninhabited islands nearby. Mikael Genberg stresses that this unconventional overnight accommodation is not just a hotel but a work of art.

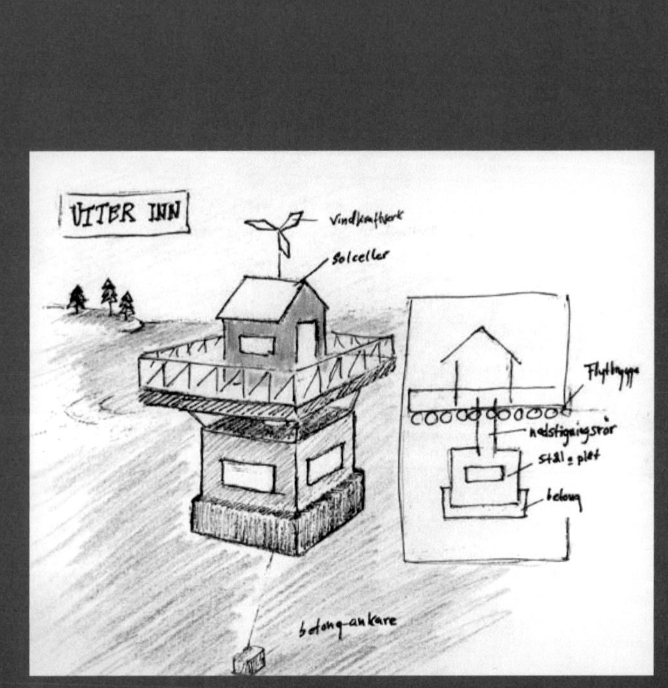

The typical Swedish cabin above the water looks cute but unimpressive. The bedroom in the steel tank suspended below is a fabulous underwater observatory.

In this final section we see water—as ice—used as a building material. Many artists, architects, and engineers are intrigued by the idea of creating temporary structures from ice. The designs in this chapter range from vernacular dwellings to a hotel to playful, artistic spaces, and even to walk-in sculptures by renowned artists. The concept of course goes back to the Inuit and their dome-shaped dwellings, as simple as they are beautiful. And just as the Inuit have numerous words for different kinds of snow, the translucency and the colors of ice and snow are widely varied: from translucent to transparent, snow with all its shades of white, ice in infinite blues and greens. These color and light effects can be used as a fine design tool, although it has to be said that photographs can never truly capture their essence. Anyone who has breathed in the scent of snow and ice cannot resist the magical radiance that emanates from these unique substances.

Frozen Hard

1234

Igloo

The Inuit igloo is a dome of snow that bears its own weight. It is a masterpiece of cultural history on a par with the cupolas of classical antiquity. The Inuit are a people of hunters and gatherers who live in the northern Polar Regions, mainly Alaska, Canada, and Greenland. The more familiar name Eskimo is actually a derogatory term coined by Native American Indians meaning "eaters of raw flesh."

Igloos are primarily temporary shelters for hunters. They can be built quickly, providing that the snow is firm enough. Fifteen to thirty-centimeter-thick blocks are cut from the firm snow with antler saws and layered in a spiral, using blocks of ever decreasing size until the spiral closes, forming an evenly rounded dome. Finally, the joints are sealed with more powdery snow and the structure is smoothed. Tiny apertures provide ventilation. A piece of ice forms a window. A typical igloo for hunters and travelers has a diameter of between three and five meters, and can accommodate three people.

The entrance to an igloo is a tunnel constructed low enough to keep out a polar bear; set lower than the living area, with its animal skin flooring, it forms a cold trap. Thanks to the insulating qualities of snow, the interior is remarkably warm and cozy. Heated only by body warmth and whale oil lamps, the temperature inside is between 4 and 8 °C (between 39 and 46 °F). The Davis Strait Inuit also cover the interior walls with animal skins, increasing the temperature to almost 20 °C (68 °F). The frozen meltwater transforms the fragile dome of snow into a sturdy ice structure capable of withstanding any storm.

Some Inuit, such as the Copper Inuit of Victoria Island, also use igloos as permanent housing. They link separate igloos to form a house with several rooms. For assemblies, there are large community huts for up to a hundred people.

In the northern Polar Regions, igloos serve as temporary shelters for the Inuit. The lower-level entrance tunnel prevents intrusion by wild animals and at the same time acts as an insulating trench to keep the warm air inside.

Without the complex calculus of structural engineering, the Inuit developed the brilliant principle of a snow dome that can bear its own weight: the igloo. Igloo is the Inuit word for house, especially houses of earth or animal skins, and has become synonymous with houses of snow.

Heinz Isler

Ice Experiments, Since 1955

The Swiss engineer Heinz Isler started experimenting with ice just a few years after graduating from university. He made a name for himself with his experimental design methods and his use of thin-walled concrete molding, while his close studies of nature taught him to determine the "natural" form. He would hang nets, cloth, strings, and balloons on trees, and support them from below with rods. They took on their natural form through their own weight and the wind. Sprayed with water, they iced over and formed self-supporting structures. Often, a millimeter-thick layer of ice was enough to allow the supporting structure to be removed. The sheer scope of this fantastic ice architecture is quite astonishing. Depending on the initial structure, the temperature, and whether the water is sprayed on manually or automatically, a huge variety of forms and structures are created. Even the subsequent melting of the thin shells of ice is a source of interesting structural engineering findings.

At night, when they are illuminated by artificial light, these forms are particularly impressive and have an almost fairytale quality. What is more, these whimsical experiments are so affordable that they are simply waiting to be imitated—enjoy!

Inflated balloons, various fabrics, and nets are sprayed with water to create these fantastic ice forms during a cold winter night.

Åke Larsson

Icehotel, Jukkasjärvi, Sweden, Annually since 1989

Restful sleep at –5 °C (23 °F)—that's the promise of the Icehotel in Jukkasjärvi in northern Sweden. And that's relatively warm and cozy, when you consider that the outside temperature can drop to –40 °C (–40 °F). For sixteen years now, in early winter (the end of October) an entire hotel is built of snow and ice, growing bigger and more spectacular each year. In the winter of 2001–02 a total of 30,000 tons of snow and 4,000 tons of ice were used to create the structure; fourteen thousand guests—in cozily warm sleeping bags—spent the night in beds made of ice and snow and covered with reindeer skins. Amongst the sixty rooms in the hotel, there are also a number of extravagantly designed deluxe suites, with special decorative ice sculptures and hot lingonberry juice, brought to the guest's bedside in the morning.

Before retiring for the night, guests can visit the Absolut Icebar for a drink "in the rocks"—in glasses made of ice from the crystal clear ice of the fast-flowing River Torne. In the Ice Chapel mass is held, children are baptized, and some guests even make their wedding vows. The hall of pillars and the cinema possess the same magic that captivates guests as they enter the hotel. From snow and ice blocks weighing up to two tons, sculptors cut windows, doors, pillars, furniture, lamps, and of course the countless sculptures that adorn all parts of the hotel. A recent addition to this magical landscape is the Ice Globe Theatre, a replica of Shakespeare's Globe Theatre in England. Like the rest of the hotel, the Theatre is made entirely of ice from the River Torne, which each spring returns to river, leaving only the memory—of a fairytale.

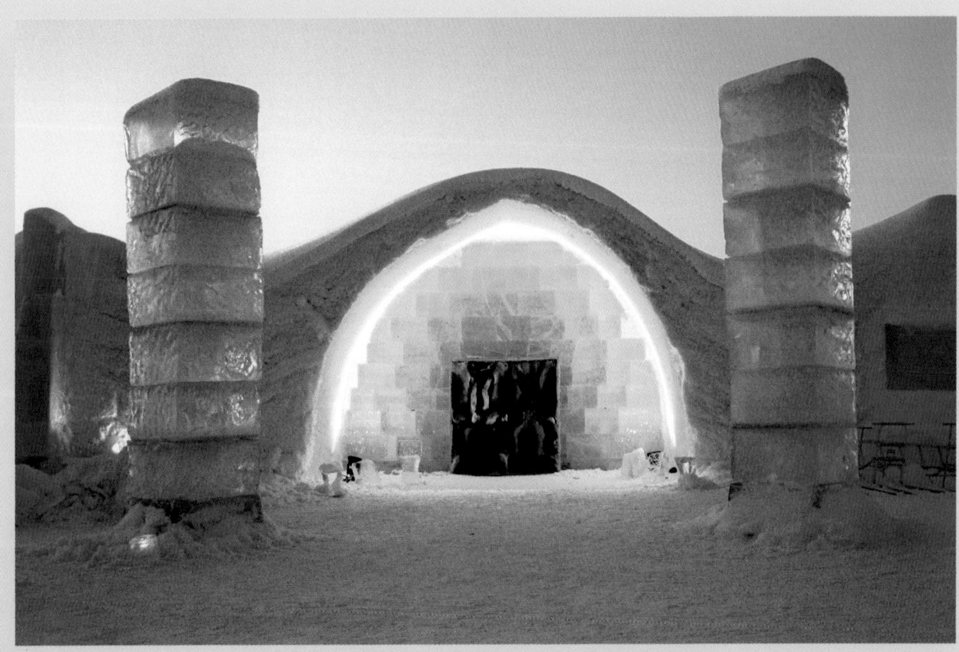

Each year for the last sixteen years, a new hotel has been constructed north of the Polar Circle—made entirely of snow and ice. Even the cocktails in the Icebar are served in crystal clear ice glasses.

Åke Larsson
Icehotel, Jukkasjärvi, Sweden, Annually since 1989

Images of a winter wonderland of pure ice and snow. Every year, thousands of guests stay at this ice palace, enjoying the many quirky details made possible by the unlimited creative potential of using frozen water as a design material.

Vienna University of Technology, Institute for Structural Engineering

Ice Domes, Project, 2004

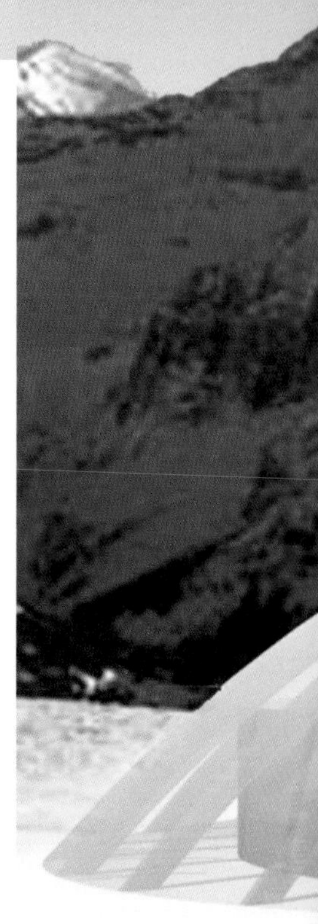

In winter, when the snow covers houses, streets, and fields in a blanket of white, the landscape briefly returns to its natural, untouched state. Yet until now, there has been no architecture appropriate to these snowy surroundings. This may well be set to change. An Austrian team headed by Johann Kollegger from the Vienna University of Technology has devised a process to create domes of fiberglass-reinforced ice for winter sports areas. These variable-sized domes can be used as shelters at ski lift stations, as snack bars, and even as venues for a whole assortment of events from concerts to film screenings.

The method was initially tested using steel-reinforced concrete. Concrete, like ice, is an extremely malleable and fluid material that can withstand high pressure, but has little tensile strength. In order to compensate this with little in the way of additional reinforcement, the designers came up with a form that generates forces of pressure rather than tension: a dome of prefabricated components that is gradually built up by tightening a prestressing element. The same process was then applied using ice. The form of the individual components was precisely calculated by computer and a fiberglass fabric was inserted to absorb the tensile stress. The experiment was a success. Hydraulic pumps were used to tighten a straining ring, creating a three-dimensional dome from the two-dimensional basic form within thirty minutes.

The completed ice dome is an inherently stable structure that allows windows and entrance openings to be cut as required. Special lighting effects can be created by freezing light conductors into the ice, illuminating enclosed bubbles and fault lines. The ice can even be dyed using food colorings—so children can cut themselves an ice pop straight out of the dome.

A process for building ice domes, developed by a team at the Vienna University of Technology, heralds the possibility of futuristic ice architecture in winter sports areas. These are temporary structures that melt in summer.

The Snow Show

Steven Holl and Jene Highstein, Oblong Voidspace, Rovaniemi, Finland, 2003

In winter, the Gulf of Bothnia freezes over so solidly that heavy goods traffic can cross the ice. The boundary between land and sea disappears beneath a blanket of snow and daylight lasts only a few hours. It was in this snowbound Finnish wilderness at the edge of the Arctic Circle that New York curator Lance Fung organized one of the most extraordinary exhibition projects of the new century in the towns of Rovaniemi and Kemi.

Rovaniemi, the capital of Lapland, perhaps best known as the home of Santa Claus, was destroyed by the Germans in the Second World War and rebuilt by architect Alvar Aalto. Kemi is famous for its Snow Castle, made of ice and built anew each year, which inspired Fung's project.

Teams, each consisting of an artist and an architect, or firm of architects, were asked to design experimental works—featuring video, audio, light, or objects—made of up to 80 percent ice and snow. Fung invited internationally renowned artist duos, among them Jene Highstein / Steven Holl, Osmo Rauhala / Asymptote, Cai Guo-Qiang / Zaha Hadid, Lothar Hempel / Studio Granda, Yoko Ono / Arata Isozaki, Eva Rothschild/Anamorphosis, Carsten Höller / Williams & Tsien, Tatsuo Miyajima / Tadao Ando, and Rachel Whiteread / Juhani Pallasmaa.

In all, more than sixty artists, designers, and architects from twenty-four different countries teamed up to create unparalleled environmental art of ice and snow—an auspicious sign of cultural cooperation.

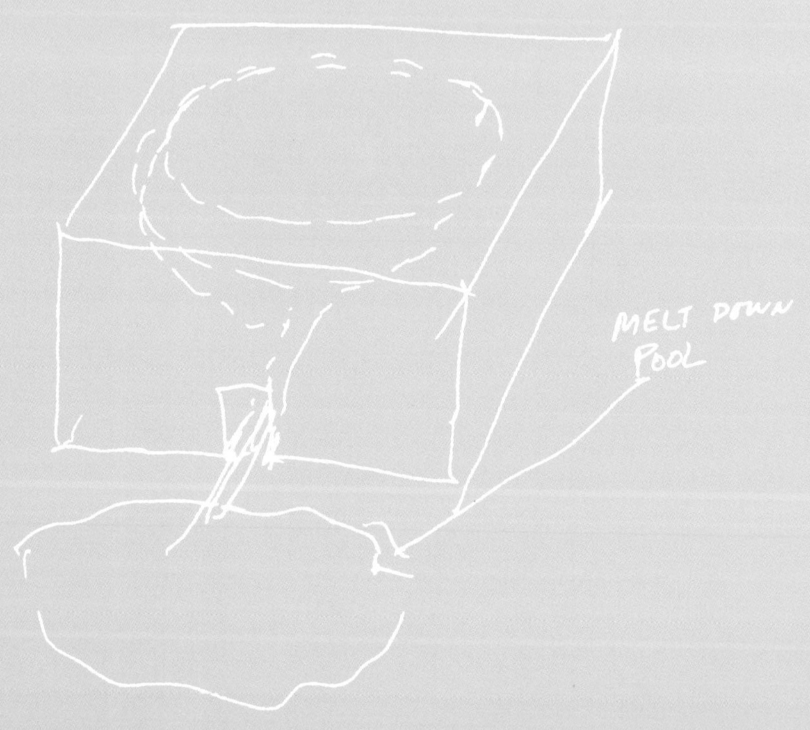

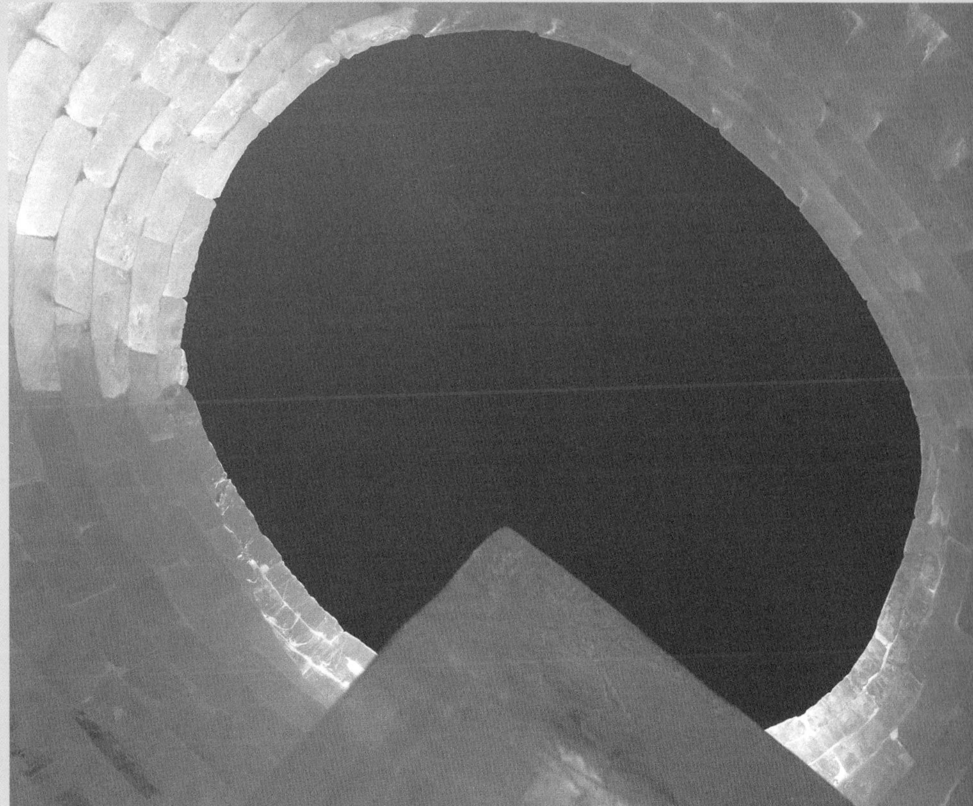

As a pilot project and preview for his groundbreaking show in 2004, New York curator Lance Fung invited American architect Steven Holl and American artist Jene Highstein to create an object together. They came up with an illuminated cube of ice in which, at night, you can see the people moving around the interior from outside.

The Snow Show
Zaha Hadid and Cai Guo-Qiang, Kemi, Finland 2004

The glacier-colored cube of ice, *Oblong Voidspace*, designed by the American duo Steven Holl and Jene Highstein for Snow Show 2003—as a pilot project for 2004— is quite subdued. At night, the angular structure with its interior rotunda radiates in a cold blue-white light that clearly illuminates the outlines of the ice blocks and reveals the figures of the visitors inside. Steven Holl, whose designs include the Museum of Contemporary Art in Helsinki, is known for his lyrical architecture. He and minimalist artist Jene Highstein sought to create a kind of primordial, cell-like human dwelling in which the transition from exterior to interior is experienced as a ceremonial act. The building has an entrance, but no roof or windows. At night, the starry sky becomes the roof, and the spring sun shining on the south side of the building will eventually create a window.

Iraqi architect and Pulitzer Prize-winner Zaha Hadid created two mirror-image landscape formations, one of snow and one of ice, an architectural fragment reminiscent of a huge piece of furniture. Chinese performance artist Cai Guo-Qiang doused the frosty sculpture in vodka and set it alight, transforming it into a shimmering blue sea of flames.

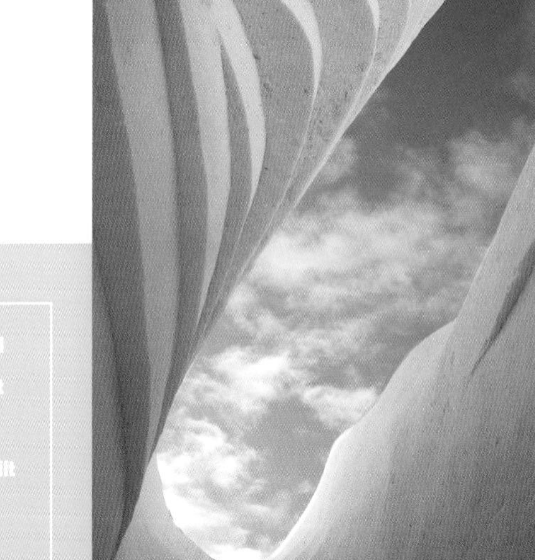

"When we started, the technology of building with ice was still in the Ice Age," quipped one of Zaha Hadid's co-workers in the early stages of the project. The artists had to set about studying the properties of this unfamiliar building material before creating their designs in snow, ice, and freezing water. Walls of ice cannot be cast, but have to be built up slowly, preferably from bottom to top, so that any air can escape. Creating clear ice glass is particularly challenging, as it requires fresh water and additional equipment.

Asymptote and Osmo Rauhala, Absolute Zero: A Lighthouse of Temporality, Kemi, Finland 2003

The snow building by New York architect Lise Anne Couture and Hani Rashid appears to oscillate. The walls soar vertically, dropping suddenly, only to balance out gradually in a gentle curve. The forms of this thirty-meter-long and seven-meter-high building are of breathtaking boldness. They recall the visualization of mathematical formulae rendered on a computer screen by software programs. Inside the dome, Finnish artist Osmo Rauhala projects videos onto the white wall of snow. The architects, who have been operating under the descriptive name of Asymptote since 1989, achieved fame with their digital projects and ludic conceptual ideas. Even the title of their snow architecture, *Absolute Zero: A Lighthouse of Temporality*, harbors a pun, referring as it does both to temperature and to mathematical coordinates.

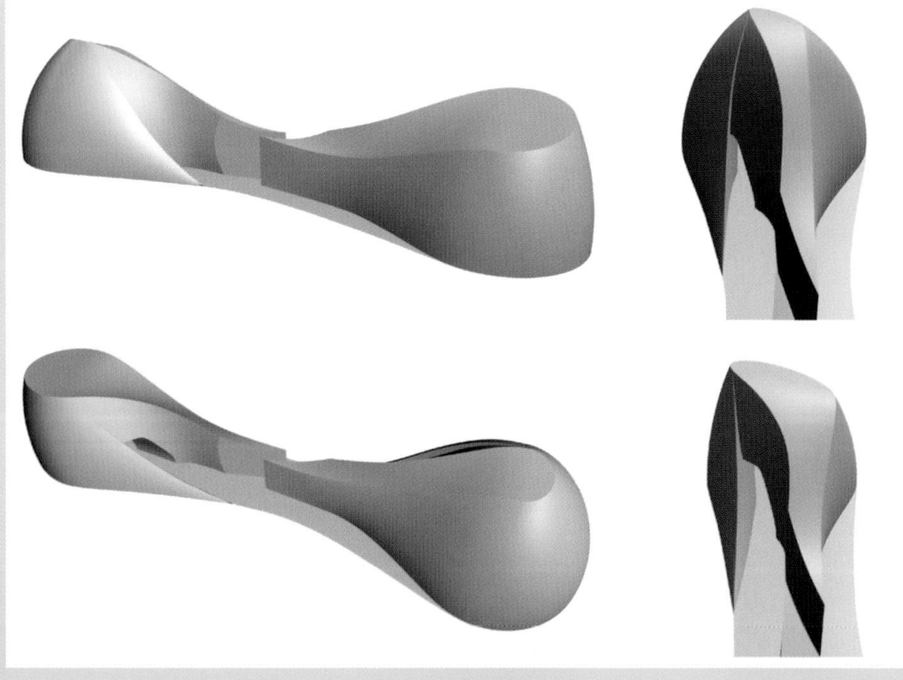

The New York group of architects Asymptote built a boldly curved structure with two domes for the Snow Show in 2003. Videos by Finnish artist Osmo Rauhala are projected on the snow wall inside. This snow building is gradually melted on the outside by the sun and on the inside by the heat of the projectors.

Selected Bibliography

Bouwen met Water. Wormer: V+K Publishing, 2003.

Flanagan, Barbara. *The Houseboat Book.* New York: Universe Publishing, 2003.

Gabor, Mark. *House Boats—Living on the Water Around the World.* New York: Random House, 1979.

Hollander, Franklin. *Hausboote – Houseboats – Woonbooten in Amsterdam.* Wiesbaden and Berlin: Bauverlag, 1983.

Lim, CJ and Ed Liu. *Realms of Impossibility Water.* Chichester: Wiley-Academy, 2002.

Loftboats. Antwerp: Tectum Publishers, 2003.

Oliver, Paul. *Dwellings.* London: Phaidon, 2003.

Rougerie, Jacques and Edith Vignes. *Habiter la Mer.* Éditions Maritime et d'Outre-Mer, 1978.

Schwartz-Claus, Mathias and Alexander von Vegesack. *Living In Motion – Design and Architecture for Flexible Dwelling.* Weil am Rhein: Vitra Design Stiftung, 2002.

Smith, Courtenay and Sean Topham. *Xtreme Houses.* Munich: Prestel, 2002.

Venhuizen, Ed. *Amphibious Living.* Rotterdam: NAI Publishers, 2000.

ViA arquitectura. Agua / Water. Alicante: Colegio Oficial de Arquitectos de la Comunidad Valenciana, December 2001.

Voigt, Wolfgang. *Atlantropa – Weltbauen am Mittelmeer. Ein Architektentraum der Moderne.* Hamburg: Dölling and Galitz Verlag, 1998.

Wilson, Anthony. *Aqua Tecture.* London: Architectural Press, 1986.

WEBSITES

www.anthenea.com

www.aquagallery.com

www.architekten-ft.de

www.bfi.org

www.cerveraandpioz.com

www.cuypers-q.be

www.floatinghomes.de

www.freedomship.com

www.giancarlozema.com

www.gmp-architetken.de

www.hertzberger.nl

www.hybrid-highrise.com

www.hydropoplis.com

www.icehotel.com

www.isler-heinz.ch

www.jul.com

www.kikutake.co.jp

www.klunderarchitecten.nl

www.lemeridien.com

www.mikaelgenberg.com

www.michadehaas.nl

www.meeresmuseum.de

www.mvrdv.nl

www.n55.dk

www.rohmer.nl

www.rougerie.com

www.schumanndesign.de

www.sea-hotel.com

www.sea-space.de

www.softroom.com

www.statoil.com

www.thepalm.co.ae

www.thesnowshow.net

www.tools-off.com

www.tuwien.ac.at/forschung/nachrichten/a-kuppelbau.html

www.wasserstadt.de

www.waterfrontmuseum.org

www.waterproof2000.be

www.waterstudio.nl

www.zeidlerpartnership.com

www.zodiacsolas.com

www.zoppini.fr

Felix Flesche is a freelancer architect and furniture designer.

Christian Burchard teaches at the University of Applied Arts in Munich and freelances for museums and galleries.

Front cover: Softroom, Floating Retreat, see pp. 86–9

Frontispiece: Jennifer Siegal, Hydra 21, 2004

Prestel Verlag
Königinstrasse 9
80539 Munich
Tel. +49 (89) 38 17 09-0
Fax +49 (89) 38 17 09-35
www.prestel.de

Prestel Publishing Ltd.
4, Bloomsbury Place
London WC1A 2QA
Tel. +44 (20) 73 23-5004
Fax +44 (20) 76 36-8004

Prestel Publishing
900 Broadway, Suite 603
New York, NY 10003
Tel. +1 (212) 995-2720
Fax +1 (212) 995-2733
www.prestel.com

Library of Congress Control Number: 2005900652

The Deutsche Bibliothek holds a record of this publication in the Deutsche Nationalbibliografie; detailed bibliographical data can be found under http://dnb.ddb.de

Prestel books are available worldwide. Please contact your nearest bookseller or one of the above addresses for information concerning your local distributor.

Translated from the German by Ishbel Flett except for the following pages by Fiona Elliott (pp. 8–18, 44, 98, 122)

Editorial direction: Angeli Sachs, Sandra Leitte
Copyediting: Jonathan Fox
Design, layout and typesetting: WIGEL, Munich
Origination: Reproline Genceller, Munich
Printing and binding: sellier, Freising

Printed in Germany on acid-free paper
ISBN 3-7913-3280-5

Picture Credits

p. 8 right: Jürg Waldmeier, Zürich
p. 9 left: Harry Schiffer, Graz
p. 10 right: Cinetext, Frankfurt
p. 11 left: Deutsches Museum, Munich; right: The World
p. 12 right: Bildagentur Huber/Gräfenhain
p. 13 right: Wildstock, Ocala, FL
p. 14 left: Royal Pavilion, Libraries and Museums (Brighton and Hove)
p. 15 left: Cinetext, Frankfurt; right: GM Media Archive
p. 16 left: Philippe Ruault
p. 17 right: Foreign Office Architects
pp. 20–21: Statoil/NN
pp. 24–25: Rob 't Hart, Rotterdam
pp. 26–27: Wilem Franken, Arnheim
p. 30: Droog Design
p. 31: Hoogstad Architecten
pp. 36–37 top: David Schleinkofer
pp. 38–39: Le Meridien Hotels and Resorts
pp. 40–43: Nakheel LLC
pp. 47: Andrew Garn, New York
pp. 48–49: Kristien Daem, Ghent
p. 50: Ilze Quaeyhaegens
p. 51: Toon Coussement
pp. 68–69: Dieter Zimmer, Hamburg
p. 76–77: Zodiac-Kern GmbH
pp. 110–113: Albi Serfaty
p. 114–115: Courtesy The Estate of R. Buckminster Fuller
pp. 116–117: Deutsches Meeresmuseum, Stralsund
pp. 124–127: Bryan & Cherry Alexander Photography
pp. 130–131, 132 top, 133: Jan Jordan, Bromma
p. 132 bottom left: Tomas Utsi, Kiruna; bottom right: Peter Grant, London
p. 136–141: Courtesy The Snow Show
p. 136 left, 137, 141: Manne Stenros
p. 138 top: Camille Mousette; bottom: Jeffrey Debany